Financial Consumer Protection in Ireland

A REVIEW OF THE CENTRAL BANK OF IRELAND'S SUPERVISORY FUNCTIONS

OECD
BETTER POLICIES FOR BETTER LIVES

Please cite this publication as:
OECD (2024), *Financial Consumer Protection in Ireland: A Review of the Central Bank of Ireland's Supervisory Functions*, OECD Publishing, Paris, https://doi.org/10.1787/5315c3ca-en.

ISBN 978-92-64-92405-5 (print)
ISBN 978-92-64-42072-4 (PDF)
ISBN 978-92-64-72422-8 (HTML)

Photo credits: Cover © PierreOlivierClementMantion/Getty Images.

Corrigenda to OECD publications may be found at: https://www.oecd.org/en/publications/support/corrigenda.html.

Preface

The Central Bank of Ireland's founding legislation set out that our constant and predominant aim would be the welfare of the people as a whole. We serve the public interest by maintaining monetary and financial stability while ensuring that the financial system operates in the best interests of consumers and the wider economy. Ultimately, everything that we do is about protecting consumers.

Over the last decade, the consumer protection framework in Ireland has been strengthened significantly, built on the foundations of the global standard, the G20/OECD High-Level Principles on Financial Consumer Protection (the FCP Principles). But as the financial services sector evolves, so too must our framework to ensure it is fit for purpose. That is why we commissioned the review by the OECD of our consumer protection supervisory functions.

The OECD's review has been a valuable opportunity for these functions to be assessed against global standards by an independent, objective third party. The findings will sit alongside our new regulatory and supervisory framework and our forthcoming new Consumer Protection Code and ensure regulated firms are operating under a modernised set of rules and approaches.

I welcome the OECD's assessment that the Central Bank is operating in line with the FCP Principles. Our Strategy recognises that we are facing a future of complexity and uncertainty and that we need to be adaptive and responsive in the way we work, building on our strong foundations. I support the OECD's recommendations on how we can further enhance our approach, in particular the insights on international best practice and peer comparisons, which we will consider carefully. I also welcome the OECD's focus on the consumer perspective, how we can further strengthen the way in which we engage with and listen to consumers, the way in which we provide them with information, and ultimately how we measure our effectiveness in terms of outcomes.

I want to acknowledge the contributions provided by our stakeholders which have informed the OECD's recommendations. Hearing their views and perspectives is important to ensure we are effective in our role. I appreciate the time they have given to this review in meeting with the OECD team and supporting their analysis.

Finally, I would like to express my appreciation to the OECD and its review team for carrying out this important piece of work. It reinforces our commitment to continuous improvement and our openness to learning so that we can continue to deliver on our constant and predominant aim in a rapidly-changing world.

Gabriel Makhlouf,

Governor, Central Bank of Ireland

Foreword

Financial consumer protection aims to ensure fair treatment of financial consumers, to promote the provision of accurate and honest information about financial products and services, and to ensure products are designed to meet the interests and objectives of consumers. It also aims to guarantee that financial services providers act responsibly and in the best interest of consumers, and to ensure consumers have access to adequate redress mechanisms when needed. Financial consumer protection plays an important role, alongside financial inclusion and financial literacy, in supporting financial resilience and the well-being of individuals, families and communities, financial stability and, ultimately, sustainable and inclusive growth.

This report sets out the findings of the review of the financial consumer protection supervisory functions of the Central Bank of Ireland. The review was conducted against the G20/OECD High-level Principles on Financial Consumer Protection, the international standard for financial consumer protection. OECD Financial Consumer Protection reviews offer countries and/or public authorities a comprehensive assessment of their financial consumer protection framework based on original analysis and international practices. The main output of this review is a set of recommendations tailored to the specific situation and needs of the Central Bank of Ireland and designed to function as a guiding tool to further strengthen its financial consumer protection supervisory functions.

To carry out the review, the OECD conducted research and met with relevant stakeholders. The review was developed by the OECD in close co-operation with the Central Bank and the OECD benefitted from inputs and discussions with relevant teams of the Central Bank and relevant Irish public authorities, and representatives of consumers and industry.

The review was prepared by Tommaso Majer under the oversight of Miles Larbey, Head of the Financial Consumer Protection, Education and Inclusion Unit and Serdar Çelik, Head of the Capital Markets and Financial Institutions Division within the OECD Directorate for Financial and Enterprise Affairs. Matthew Soursourian also from the Financial Consumer Protection, Education and Inclusion Unit provided valuable comments. Editorial and communication support was provided by Liv Gudmundson, Thomas Dannequin, Eva Abbott and Flora Monsaingeon-Lavuri. Katerina Kodlova provided support to the project.

Table of contents

INFOGRAPHICS

TABLES

BOXES

Executive summary

Effective financial consumer protection helps ensuring that individuals can participate in the financial system with safeguards against unfair practices, frauds and exploitation. Financial consumer protection is essential to prevent over indebtedness, ensure transparency in financial products and empower consumers to make informed decisions.

This report presents the findings of the review of the financial consumer protection supervisory functions of the Central Bank of Ireland (Central Bank). The review assesses the alignment of these functions with the G20/OECD High-Level Principles on Financial Consumer Protection (FCP Principles), the international standard for financial consumer protection. The review also identifies areas for improvement and sets out a series of recommendations.

Key findings

The Central Bank's financial consumer protection supervisory functions are well aligned with the G20/OECD High-Level Principles on Financial Consumer Protection.

The Central Bank is a mature and sophisticated oversight body and has appropriate policies and practices in place to effectively monitor financial markets, identify risks to consumers and improve outcomes for consumers. The Central Bank plays a crucial role in overseeing Ireland's financial markets and ensuring their proper functioning by promoting transparency, fairness, and trust.

The Central Bank is strongly committed to fostering and upholding the G20/OECD High-Level Principles on Financial Consumer Protection.

The Central Bank's strong commitment to fostering and upholding the FCP Principles reflects its recognition of the increasingly global and interconnected nature of financial markets, where consumers engage with a wide and growing range of products and services. To ensure that consumers are adequately protected, the Central Bank aligns its policies and practices with the FCP Principles, it meets the expectations outlined by the FCP Principles, and its practices are consistent with the practices of its peer oversight bodies.

The Central Bank is committed to transforming its approach to supervision.

As the financial services industry has undergone, and continues to undergo, significant transformation due to a combination of rapid technological innovation and changes in macroeconomic conditions, the Central Bank is committed to transforming its approach to supervision. Technological and macroeconomic changes have fundamentally altered the landscape in which financial consumer protection oversight bodies operate, presenting both new opportunities and challenges. Advancements in financial technology, such as digital payments, have revolutionised the way financial services are delivered to consumers. While these innovations provide consumers with greater convenience, access, and efficiency, they also introduce new risks. At the same time, the higher interest rate environment has increased the cost of borrowing for consumers and may lead to financial strain for those with significant debt obligations.

In this changing landscape, the Central Bank, in its 2021 Strategic Plan, sets out the commitment to transforming its approach to supervision so that it continues to be well-positioned to meet its objective of ensuring consumers of financial services are protected in all respects in a changing and increasingly complex and interconnected financial landscape.

The Central Bank could further strengthen its financial consumer protection supervisory functions in some areas.

While the Central Bank's policies and practices are well aligned with the FCP Principles, it could further strengthen its financial consumer protection supervisory functions to support its transformation and accelerate the evolution of its risk-based supervisory approach. Delivered in conjunction with an integrated supervisory approach, these improvements would help the Central Bank drive ever better outcomes for consumers.

Recommendations

The recommendations of the review are grouped under six themes:

- Theme 1. **Ensuring consumers continue to be protected as part of the Central Bank's integrated supervisory approach**. As the Central Bank evolves its framework to deliver a more integrated approach to supervision across its overall mandate, and complemented by a revised operating structure, it should ensure consumers continue to be protected as part of its new integrated supervisory approach.
- Theme 2. **Measuring and demonstrating the effectiveness of the financial consumer protection supervisory functions of the Central Bank**. Although the Central Bank embeds a number of effectiveness checks regarding its consumer protection supervisory functions in its ways of working, it could evolve its supervisory framework by embedding an approach to assess the impact on consumer outcomes of its financial consumer protection functions.
- Theme 3. **Engaging with consumers and consumer groups**. Interviews with the Central Bank and stakeholders suggested that it may be challenging for the Central Bank to obtain the consumer perspective on the broad range of financial consumer protection matters within its remit. Therefore, the Central Bank should continue to innovate in how it engages with consumers.
- Theme 4. **Informing and educating financial consumers.** As part of Ireland's National Strategy for Financial Literacy developed by the Department of Finance, and in line with its mandate to ensure the proper and effective regulation of financial service providers and markets while ensuring that consumers of financial services are protected, the Central Bank should continue to educate and inform financial consumers.
- Theme 5. **Protecting consumers experiencing vulnerability**. Given the new requirements proposed as part of the review of the Central Bank's Consumer Protection Code, the Central Bank should continue to develop its financial consumer protection supervisory functions to ensure enhanced protection of consumers in vulnerable circumstances.
- Theme 6. **Using data in financial consumer protection supervision**. As financial markets continue to evolve and grow in complexity, the Central Bank should continue to adapt its data policies and practices.

1 Introduction

This chapter introduces the review of the financial consumer protection supervisory functions of the Central Bank of Ireland. After providing the background of the review, the chapter presents the purpose and the scope of the review, a brief overview of the G20/OECD High-Level Principles on Financial Consumer Protection, the methodology used and the structure of the report.

1.1. Background

OECD Financial Consumer Protection Assessments (FCP Assessment) offers countries and/or public authorities a comprehensive and objective assessment of their financial consumer protection framework based on original analysis, along with policy recommendations tailored to a country's specific situation and needs. The purpose of an FCP Assessment is to conduct an evidence-based review and comparative analysis against the G20/OECD High-Level Principles on Financial Consumer Protection (FCP Principles) and international practices and effective approaches in order to identify potential gaps and recommendations for areas for improvement. The recommendations may also include suggestions on how to improve FCP policies and practices based on successful measures taken in other countries.

The focus of this FCP Assessment is to review the financial consumer protection supervisory functions of the Central Bank of Ireland (Central Bank). The Central Bank's Strategy comprises four connected themes (Future-Focused, Open & Engaged, Transforming and Safeguarding) (Central Bank of Ireland, 2021[1]). These themes acknowledge that, in a rapidly changing world, the Central Bank must transform the way that it operates in order to succeed, including looking for continuous improvement in its ways of working. In line with this strategy, the Central Bank and the OECD agreed that the OECD would undertake an FCP Assessment by reviewing the financial consumer protection supervisory functions of the Central Bank of Ireland against the FCP Principles.[1]

1.2. Purpose

The purpose of this report is to set out the results of the review of the financial consumer protection supervisory functions of the Central Bank (review) by the OECD.

The review consists of a mapping of the financial consumer protection supervisory functions of the Central Bank with respect to its alignment with the FCP Principles (Chapter 2). The mapping is based on desk research including relevant legislation, regulation, institutional arrangements and data, the responses to a detailed questionnaire completed by the Central Bank and other national authorities to understand the current FCP policies and practices in Ireland, as well as fact-finding meetings between the OECD and various teams of the Central Bank, relevant national authorities and other public and private stakeholders. Chapter 3 provides an assessment of the financial consumer protection supervisory functions of the Central Bank, identifies areas for improvement and formulates recommendations. The assessment is informed by the mapping, discussions with relevant stakeholders, the FCP Principles, other relevant OECD Recommendations and other instruments and, where appropriate, international best practices and effective approaches.

1.3. Scope of the review

As described in more detail in section 2.2.2, the mandate of the Central Bank encompasses financial stability and prudential supervision as well as consumer protection. While the scope of the review is the Central Bank's financial consumer protection supervisory functions, as an integrated central bank and financial services regulator, the Central Bank's assessment of risks at system level, firm level and consumer level are also relevant. Therefore, this report also refers, where relevant, to broader aspects of the mandate of the Central Bank to understand its consumer protection supervisory functions.

For completeness and context, and where relevant, the review also considers the broader landscape of financial consumer protection policy and institutional arrangements in Ireland, even though such arrangements do not fall within the scope of the review and are not the subject of recommendations.

The paragraphs below provide a brief description of the financial services sectors that are outside the remit of the Central Bank as well the FCP Principles that are not directly applicable to the financial consumer protection supervisory functions of the Central Bank for the purpose of this review.

Firstly, the Central Bank does not have responsibility for financial consumer protection supervision of all sectors of the financial services industry. As set out in section 2.1.5, certain products that can be used for financial and investment purposes do not fall within the regulatory remit of the Central Bank. Moreover, the Central Bank does not have a central role relating to the pension markets. Occupational pension schemes and personal retirement savings accounts (which are, together with the state-supported public pension system, the three main pillars of Ireland's pensions system) are regulated by the Pensions Authority through its supervision of compliance with the Pensions Act 1990. The Central Bank authorises and supervises financial services firms who sell pension products or manage pension assets, but it does not have responsibilities relating to the supervision of the business conduct of occupational pensions schemes. These financial services firms include credit institutions, investment firms and insurance companies providing personal pension products, investment and insurance intermediaries providing advice relating to retirement savings products (including retirement phase arrangements), and investment management firms providing services relating to the assets in occupational schemes. Finally, the Central Bank is responsible for the collection of data on occupational pension schemes.

Moreover, the Health Insurance Authority is the statutory regulator of the private health insurance market under the Health Insurance Acts 1994-2015 which address access to health insurance coverage (for example through open enrolment and lifetime cover) and specify minimum levels of coverage that health insurance contracts must include. Finally, the Competition and Consumer Protection Commission is responsible for the authorisation of credit intermediaries.

Secondly, not all aspects of the FCP Principles are directly applicable to the financial consumer protection supervisory functions of the Central Bank. The Central Bank does not have a statutory function in respect of financial literacy and awareness (Principle 4) and the Competition and Consumer Protection Commission promotes compliance with and enforces competition law in Ireland (Principle 5). However, the Central Bank undertakes a number of consumer awareness initiatives, and it has an objective to ensure that financial markets function in an orderly and proper manner, and it is the competent authority for the supervision and enforcement of compliance with provisions to support consumers when switching between financial services products and firms. In addition, Principle 11 on the protection of consumer data and privacy is not directly applicable to the financial consumer protection supervisory functions of the Central Bank for the purpose of this review as the Central Bank does not have a role in supervising compliance with the Data Protection Legislation (compliance with the Data Protection Legislation is supervised and enforced by the Data Protection Commission). As a data controller, however, the Central Bank is subject to compliance with the Data Protection Legislation, and it has policies, procedures and controls in place for this purpose. Moreover, relating to Principle 12 on complaints handling and redress, the Central Bank is the competent authority for supervising that regulated firms have complaints handling procedures in place, while the Financial Services and Pensions Ombudsman holds the statutory function of independently and impartially resolving consumer complaints about the conduct of financial services providers regulated by the Central Bank and pension providers regulated by the Pensions Authority.

Furthermore, several other public authorities play an important role in Ireland's financial consumer protection landscape, such as the Department of Finance, the Insolvency Service of Ireland and *An Garda Síochána* (the national police and security service of the Republic of Ireland). Where appropriate and to ensure completeness, the review includes information about the broader financial consumer protection landscape and provides a brief description of the role of other relevant public authorities in Ireland in relation to the financial consumer protection supervisory functions of the Central Bank.

1.4. G20/OECD High-Level Principles on Financial Consumer Protection

Effective financial consumer protection is an important part of well-functioning financial markets, as it promotes responsible and fair treatment of consumers, increases trust and confidence in the financial system, and supports meaningful financial inclusion, increasing participation in financial activities, such as savings, borrowing and investing. Financial consumer protection also fosters healthy competition between financial institutions by allowing consumers to make informed decisions and choose the best products for their needs.

The FCP Principles are the international standard for comprehensive and effective financial consumer protection frameworks. Governments, oversight bodies (i.e. financial regulators and supervisors), and other relevant institutions are recommended to implement the FCP Principles at the national level.

The FCP Principles were developed by the G20/OECD Task Force on Financial Consumer Protection (Task Force) and first endorsed by G20 Leaders in November 2011 (G20 Leaders, 2011[2]) and adopted by OECD Members in the form of a Recommendation in July 2012 (OECD, 2022[3]). The FCP Principles are included in the Financial Stability Board (FSB) Compendium of Standards and referenced in the G20 Financial Inclusion Action Plan.

Over the course of 2021-22, the Task Force conducted a comprehensive review and update of the FCP Principles. The updated FCP Principles were endorsed by G20 Leaders on 15-16 November 2022 (G20 Leaders, 2022[4]) and adopted by OECD Members via a revised Recommendation on 12 December 2022.

The 2022 review of the Principles introduced three main updates: i) the addition of two new principles ("Access and Inclusion" and "Quality Financial Products"); ii) the inclusion of three cross-cutting themes relevant to the consideration and implementation of each and all of the FCP Principles ("digitalisation", "financial well-being" and "sustainable finance"); and iii) the incorporation of lessons from the response to the COVID-19 pandemic such as enhanced protections for consumers who may be vulnerable and a greater focus on tackling financial scams.

The FCP Principles underscore the importance of consumer trust and confidence in the financial system and emphasise the need for consumers to be treated fairly and responsibly in their dealings with financial service providers. Integrating consumer protection policies into regulatory frameworks strengthens financial stability and ensures fair treatment for consumers. The FCP Principles recognise the importance of financial innovation and digitalisation, enabling consumers to benefit from new opportunities while managing associated risks. Additionally, the FCP Principles address vulnerabilities that some consumers may face due to personal characteristics, behavioural biases and market conditions. Infographic 1.1. provides an overview of the FCP Principles.

Infographic 1.1. G20/OECD High-Level Principles on Financial Consumer Protection

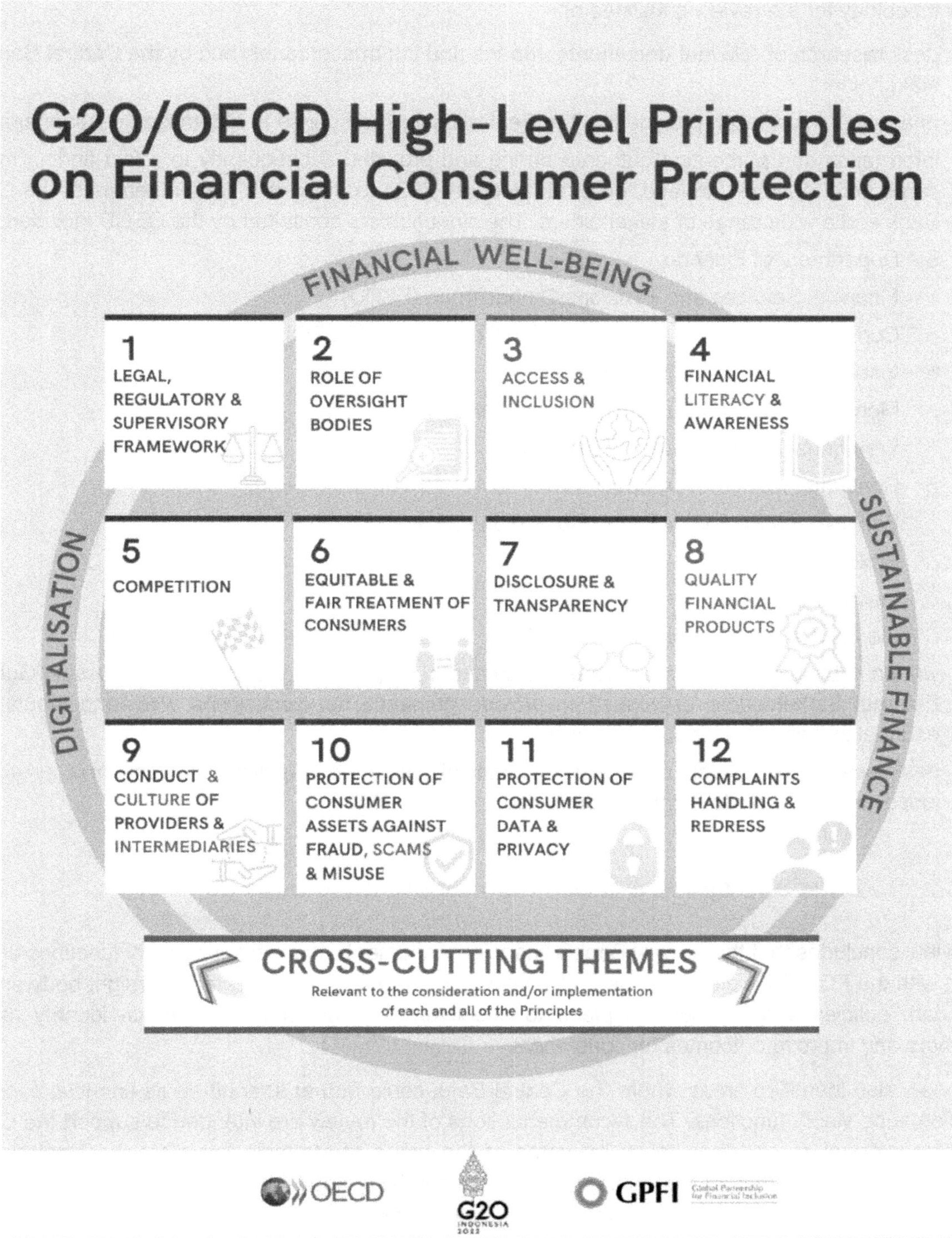

Note: Text in green colour denotes revisions made through the 2021-2022 review and update of the High-Level Principles on Financial Consumer Protection.

Source: OECD (2022[3]), G20/OECD High-Level Principles on Financial Consumer Protection, https://legalinstruments.oecd.org/en/instruments/OECD-LEGAL-0394.

1.5. Methodology

The Methodology for the review consisted of:

- desk research of relevant documents, reports and information published by the Central Bank and stakeholders,
- analysis of information provided by the Central Bank in response to a detailed questionnaire,
- information and perception gathered during and provided subsequently to a fact-finding mission carried out in Dublin, Ireland, on 22-26 January 2024 to meet with various teams of the Central Bank and a wide range of stakeholders. The stakeholders consulted by the OECD included:
    - Department of Finance
    - Financial Services and Pensions Ombudsman (FSPO)
    - Competition and Consumer Protection Commission (CCPC)
    - Insolvency Service of Ireland (ISI)
    - Money Advice and Budgeting Service (MABS)
    - Free Legal Advice Centres (FLAC)
    - Consumer Advisory Group (CAG)
    - Banking and Payments Federation Ireland (BPFI)
    - Brokers Ireland
    - Insurance Ireland
    - the Irish Banking Culture Board (IBCB).
- written submissions from stakeholders provided in response to the OECD's Discussion Guide for External Stakeholders developed to provide guidance for discussions with, and inputs from, external stakeholders about the review,
- desk research on relevant aspects of the financial consumer protection framework of other selected jurisdictions to provide points of comparison.

1.6. Key findings and detailed recommendations by theme

The review concludes that the Central Bank's financial consumer protection supervisory functions are well aligned with the FCP Principles. The Central Bank is a mature and sophisticated oversight body and has appropriate policies and practices in place to effectively monitor financial markets, identify risks to consumers and improve outcomes for consumers.

The review also identifies areas where the Central Bank could further strengthen its financial consumer protection supervisory functions. The recommendations of the review are intended to support the Central Bank's transformation and they touch on some of the areas of strategic focus for the Central Bank, including accelerating the evolution of its risk-based supervisory approach. Delivered in conjunction with an integrated supervisory approach, the recommendations represent an opportunity for the Central Bank to drive ever better outcomes for consumers. Drawing on the mapping set out in Chapter 2 as well as international experience and interviews with representatives of the Central Bank and other relevant Irish institutions, Chapter 3 presents the assessment of the financial consumer protection supervisory functions of the Central Bank and identifies areas for improvements. This section lists the recommendations for each of these areas.

1.6.1. Theme 1 - Ensuring consumers continue to be protected as part of the Central Bank's integrated supervisory approach

In evolving its framework to deliver a more integrated supervisory approach, the Central Bank should:

- Ensure that its governance and supervisory structures retain explicit consumer and investor protection objectives, to make retail financial markets deliver good outcomes for consumers.

1.6.2. Theme 2 - Measuring and demonstrating the effectiveness of the financial consumer protection supervisory functions of the Central Bank

The Central Bank should:

- Build on existing initiatives to embed the evaluation of the effectiveness of its financial consumer protection supervisory activities on consumer outcomes in its supervisory framework.
- Assess and review the effectiveness of "Dear CEO" letters as a supervisory tool.

1.6.3. Theme 3 – Engaging with consumers and consumer groups

The Central Bank should:

- Enhance the Consumer Advisory Group (CAG) to ensure that it includes the consumer perspective on the broad range of financial consumer protection matters within the remit of the Central Bank. This could be done, for example, by reserving some space on the CAG for representatives of consumers or consumer associations. This would build on the valuable role that the CAG already plays in advising the Central Bank and would help the CAG to provide a broader view of the Irish consumer experience.
- Conduct periodic surveys of Ireland's adult population to evaluate and track consumer behaviours and attitudes towards financial products and services and to build consumer segmentation models.
- Conduct more regular engagement with small businesses in their capacity as consumers of financial services. This could be done, for example, by including representatives of small businesses in the current structure for consumer engagement.

1.6.4. Theme 4 – Informing and educating financial consumers

Recognising that the Central Bank does not have an explicit statutory function relating to financial literacy and awareness, and in line with its mandate to ensure the proper and effective regulation of financial service providers and markets while ensuring that consumers of financial services are protected, the Central Bank should:

- Continue to collaborate and co-ordinate with other stakeholders on the development and implementation of the forthcoming National Strategy for Financial Literacy. This is important to share information and best practices across stakeholders, avoid duplication and use resources efficiently.
- Consider the use of financial literacy as a supervisory tool and conduct initiatives aimed at increasing consumers' awareness about their rights when dealing with financial services providers, for example by enhancing the Central Bank's Consumer Hub.
- Ensure that communication to consumers about financial scams and frauds remains a priority, given the increasing prevalence of scams and frauds in Ireland (as in many other jurisdictions).
- Continue to identify and seek to address impediments to consumers switching financial products (taking into account the potential benefits for consumers).

1.6.5. Theme 5 – Protecting consumers experiencing vulnerability

Given new requirements proposed as part of the review of the Consumer Protection Code (Code), the Central Bank should:

- Focus on the implementation of the new provisions of the Code by
  - developing a supervisory approach to ensure that financial services providers adapt to the new requirements and that consumers in vulnerable circumstances are treated fairly, and
  - clarifying to financial services providers how the Central Bank views their treatment of consumers in vulnerable circumstances from a risk tolerance perspective.
- Develop an evidence-based understanding of consumer vulnerability by undertaking research to identify the main drivers of vulnerability for Irish financial consumers and their prevalence. This could be done, for example, by including relevant questions in the survey about consumer behaviour and attitudes towards financial products and services of Ireland's adult population.
- Ensure regulated financial services providers continue to support consumers, especially those in vulnerable circumstances, during the digital transformation to make sure that digital tools and practices are designed and implemented with a consumer focus.

1.6.6. Theme 6 – Using data in financial consumer protection supervision

The Central Bank should:

- Continue to ensure that all information collected for financial consumer protection supervisory purposes adheres to data and governance standards in line with the wider Central Bank Data Strategy. This information should be used alongside data more broadly already available to the Central Bank and assessed to be relevant to identifying and articulating consumer protection risks. The combined sources should be presented in an easily accessible, consistent, usable, and digestible manner for relevant supervisory teams so that it can support the Central Bank's consumer protection supervisory functions in an efficient manner on an ongoing basis.
- Ensure that the functionality necessary to support the Central Bank's financial consumer protection supervisory functions is identified and incorporated in the single supervisory workbench throughout all stages of its evolution.
- Where necessary, continue to make targeted additions and refinements to the data that the Central Bank collects from financial services providers on an ongoing basis, in order to inform the Central Bank's financial consumer protection supervisory functions on a firm-specific, sectoral or cross sectoral basis.
- Continue to invest in staff training so that supervisory teams with responsibility for financial consumer protection supervision evolve their knowledge and abilities in order to support their use of the enhanced tools and increased data available to them.
- Continue to enhance the way in which data from the Central Credit Register (CCR) is used. CCR data could provide insights on risks to consumers, enhancing the Central Bank's risk identification capabilities and complement consumer research, subject to compliance with the requirements of the Credit Reporting Act and data protection legislation.

1.7. Structure of the report

The report is structured as follows:

- Chapter 2 provides the mapping of the financial consumer protection supervisory functions of the Central Bank as of the beginning of November 2024

- Chapter 3 presents the assessment of the financial consumer protection supervisory functions of the Central Bank and the recommendations.

References

Central Bank of Ireland (2021), *Our Strategy*. [1]

G20 Leaders (2022), *2022 Leaders' Declaration*. [4]

G20 Leaders (2011), *G20 Leaders Summit*. [2]

OECD (2022), *G20/OECD High-Level Principles on Financial Consumer Protection*, https://legalinstruments.oecd.org/en/instruments/OECD-LEGAL-0394 (accessed on 10 March 2024). [3]

OECD (2022), *Recommendation of the Council on High-Level Principles on Financial Consumer Protection*, https://legalinstruments.oecd.org/en/instruments/OECD-LEGAL-0394. [5]

Note

[1] The Central Bank is also required to make arrangements for a review of the performance of its regulatory functions at least every four years and the review is intended to meet this requirement in respect of the Central Bank's consumer protection supervisory functions.

2 Mapping of the financial consumer protection supervisory functions of the Central Bank of Ireland

This chapter maps the financial consumer protection supervisory functions of the Central Bank of Ireland against the G20/OECD High-Level Principles on Financial Consumer Protection. For each principle, the chapter provides a brief description of the principle and outlines the role of the Central Bank, relevant standards and requirements, and the Central Bank's practices and activities relating to the implementation of the principle as of the beginning of November 2024.

2.1. Principle 1: Legal, Regulatory and Supervisory Framework

Principle 1 states that financial consumer protection should be an integral part of the legal, regulatory and supervisory framework. Financial consumer protection should be comprehensive, cover all financial products and services and should reflect the diversity of national circumstances and global market and regulatory developments within the financial sector. Regulation needs to be tailored and proportionate to the characteristics, risks and variety of financial products, services, providers and consumers and it should be responsive to evolving technology and delivery channels and promote consumers' financial well-being. There should be robust legal, judicial and supervisory mechanisms in place to safeguard consumers from misconduct, financial fraud, abuses and errors, and sanctions should be imposed when necessary. The regulatory toolkit should be flexible to effectively address emerging risks. Finally, when developing and reviewing policies, relevant governmental and non-governmental stakeholders, including industry, consumer organisations, professional bodies, and research communities must be consulted.

2.1.1. Nature of the legal, regulatory, and supervisory framework

Ireland's legal, regulatory and supervisory financial consumer protection framework comprises European Union (EU) legislation (as transposed into Irish Law), including guidelines issued by the European Supervisory Authorities (ESAs), Irish domestic legislation, the Central Bank's codes of conduct and regulations, and the Central Bank's guidance and supervisory expectations. EU legislation typically sets out either harmonised or minimum standards and provides for firms to be authorised in a single "home" Member State. Firms are then typically able to "passport" from their home Member State into other EU "host" Member States without seeking additional authorisation. Member State requirements (such as domestic legislation or Central Bank codes of conduct and regulations) set out additional consumer protection and conduct of business requirements and may also apply to a firm passporting into a host jurisdiction where EU legislation has not fully harmonised the regime.

Ireland's legal, regulatory and supervisory framework has elements of both a principles-based system, where regulated firms must comply with a set of broad principles and a rules-based system, where regulated firms need to comply with a set of detailed rules. For example, the Central Bank's Consumer Protection Code (Code) sets out the General Principles that require firms to act honestly, fairly and professionally in the best interest of its customers (see section 2.1.2 for details on the Code). Similar principles are also included in sectoral legislation such as MiFID II. Moreover, the Central Bank also defines consumer outcomes applying its Retail Conduct Supervisory Framework (see section 2.2.4 for details on the Central Bank's Retail Conduct Supervisory Framework) and communicating identified risks and expected consumer outcomes in its Regulatory and Supervisory Outlook (Central Bank of Ireland, 2024[1]) and other communications (such as the "Dear CEO" letters, Risk Mitigation Programmes, newsletters).

The following paragraphs provide a description of the key elements of Ireland's legal, regulatory and supervisory framework relating to financial consumer protection. The report refers to this and other legislation as appropriate, and further detail as regards the standards, requirements and guidance that address each of the FCP Principles is set out in the relevant sections below. Box 2.1 provides a brief overview of different types of firms authorised and regulated by the Central Bank that provide services to consumers.

Key legislation

This section briefly outlines the legislation under which firms are authorised and the key legislation of Ireland's legal, regulatory and supervisory framework relating to financial consumer protection. Generally, all references to legislation are to the legislation as amended up to the date of the report. It is important to note that, while the Central Bank supervises and enforces compliance with these requirements, individual firms have a responsibility to ensure that they comply with the regulatory requirements applicable to them and to meet their obligations to act in the best interests of their customers.

Consumer and mortgage credit

The Consumer Credit Act 1995 sets out requirements for the advertisement of credit, the form and content of credit agreements and provisions to protect consumers' interests during the duration of the agreement and at its termination. It also sets out requirements in relation to hire-purchase and consumer hire agreements. Finally, section 149 requires certain firms, including banks and retail credit firms, to notify the Central Bank if they wish to introduce any new customer charges or increase any existing customer charges in respect of certain services, which the Central Bank assesses against the criteria set out in that section.[1]

The European Union (Consumer Mortgage Credit Agreements) Regulations 2016 transposed into Irish Law the EU Mortgage Credit Directive. These Regulations set out requirements aimed at enhancing consumer protection in the context of residential and non-residential property credit agreements. They establish provisions concerning the transparency of credit terms, disclosure requirements and the provision of information to consumers. Additionally, they address responsible lending practices and the assessment of consumer creditworthiness, and they outline rules regarding the advertising and marketing of credit agreements. The Regulations were recently amended to expand upon the existing forbearance provisions and a list of possible measures are now included as part of that amendment. They also include provisions for mortgage credit intermediaries to assist consumers in undertaking preparatory work or other pre-contractual administration in respect of credit agreements and to conclude credit agreements on behalf of a creditor.

The European Communities (Consumer Credit Agreements) Regulations 2010 transposed into Irish Law the EU Consumer Credit Directive, and aim at enhancing consumer protection, transparency and competition in consumer credit markets. Key provisions include requirements for clear and standardised disclosure to consumers prior to entering into credit agreements, such as total cost of credit, annual percentage rate, repayment schedules and other terms and conditions. The Regulations also mandate responsible lending practices including assessing the creditworthiness of consumers before granting credit and ensuring affordability. The Regulations were recently amended to include a new regulation in relation to forbearance options and a list of possible measures are now included as part of that amendment. The revised Consumer Credit Directive will bring additional types of loans such as crowdfunding credit, interest-free credit products, certain leasing agreements and others into the scope of the EU regulatory regime, although many of these activities are already regulated under Irish law.

The Central Bank (Supervision and Enforcement) Act 2013 (Section 48) (Licensed Moneylenders) Regulations 2020 set conduct standards, disclosure obligations, and consumer protection measures for high-cost credit providers (previously known as 'moneylenders'). For example, they include the requirement that providers of high-cost credit products should take reasonable steps to identify vulnerable consumers (Central Bank of Ireland, 2021[2]). The Consumer Credit Act 1995 sets out interest rate caps on high-cost credit agreements.

The Credit Union Act 1997 established the Central Bank as the regulator of credit unions in Ireland and sets out the requirements for the establishment, governance, and operation of credit unions, including membership eligibility lending practices and financial reporting obligations.

The European Banking Authority (EBA) Guidelines on product oversight and governance arrangements for retail banking products (such as mortgages, personal loans, deposits, payment accounts, payment services and electronic money) provide a framework to ensure the effective management of retail banking products throughout their lifecycle. Key provisions include the requirement for banks to create clear procedures for the development, approval, monitoring and review of retail banking products, including identifying target markets and ensuring that products meet consumer needs. Banks are also required to have a robust governance structure to oversee product development and to integrate product oversight and governance into their overall risk management framework. The guidelines also emphasise the importance of ensuring fair treatment of consumers.

Payment Accounts and Payment Services

The European Union (Payment Accounts) Regulations 2016 transposed into Irish Law the EU Payment Accounts Directive and set out requirements about transparency and comparability of fees on payment accounts, introduce the right of access to payment accounts with basic features and other rules about switching payment accounts and to facilitate cross-border account opening.

The European Union (Payment Services) Regulations 2018 (PSR) transposed into Irish Law the EU Payment Services Directive 2 (PSD2). The PSR sets out transparency and information requirements for payment services and introduces the requirement for firms to adopt strong customer authentication to improve payment security and reduce risks of fraud. The PSR also facilitates open banking by allowing authorised third-party providers to access account information and payment initiation services, requires firms to provide clear and transparent information about payment transactions, including charges and other terms and conditions, and establishes procedures for handling consumer complaints.

Retail Investment

The European Union (Markets in Financial Instruments) Regulations 2017 (MiFID II Regulations) transposed into Irish Law the EU Markets in Financial Instruments Directive (MiFID II). These Regulations, together with the EU Markets in Financial Instruments Regulation (MiFIR), aim at enhancing investor protection, increasing transparency and promoting integrity of financial markets. Concerning financial consumer protection, this legislation requires firms to disclose costs and charges, to ensure suitability and appropriateness of investment products for consumers and to provide clear information on risks associated to the investment product. Firms are also required to manage conflicts of interest to ensure that clients' interests are protected.

The Investment Intermediaries Act 1995 (IIA) regulates the activities of investment intermediaries and, together with the requirements of the Code, sets requirements that are analogous to certain provisions of the MiFID II Regulations, including provisions relating to conduct of business in respect of their activities such as requirements relating to complaints handling, disclosure and fair treatment of clients.

The European Communities (Undertakings for Collective Investment in Transferable Securities) Regulations 2011 (UCITS Regulations), which transpose Council Directive 2009/65/EC, Commission Directive 2010/EC and Commission Directive 2010/44/EC into Irish law, set out requirements in respect of UCITS, a type of investment fund. The Central Bank (Supervision and Enforcement) Act 2013 (Section 48(1)) (Undertakings for Collective Investment in Transferable Securities) Regulations 2019 (the Central Bank UCITS Regulations) consolidate into one location all the requirements which the Central Bank imposes on UCITS, UCITS management companies and depositories of UCITS. UCITS are designed for the retail market and as such are easy for investors to understand. They are subject to disclosure, liquidity, diversification and investment limit rules.

The European Union (Alternative Investment Fund Managers) Regulations 2013 (AIFM Regulations) and the Central Bank's AIF Rulebook set out requirements for Retail Investor AIFs (RIAIFs). A RIAIF is an alternative investment fund (AIF) authorised by the Central Bank which may be marketed to retail investors. RIAIFs are subject to less investment and eligible asset restrictions than UCITS but are subject to a regime more restrictive than the regime for AIFs that may be marketed to qualifying investors.

Fund management companies are responsible for the investment management, administration and distribution of UCITS and AIFs. Fund management companies can be authorised as UCITS management companies, or Alternative Investment Fund Managers. The eligibility criteria and authorisation/approval requirements for each is set out in the UCITS Regulations and AIFM Regulations, respectively.

Insurance

The European Union (Insurance Distribution) Regulations 2018 (IDR) transposed the EU Insurance Distribution Directive (IDD) into Irish Law. The IDR regulates how insurance products are designed and distributed in Ireland and it seeks to improve consumer protection standards. More prescriptive rules apply to distributors selling insurance products that have an investment element, for example insurance-based investment products The IDR also requires insurance undertakings and distributors to implement product oversight and governance processes to ensure that recommended products are suitable to a consumers' needs and objectives. The IDR sets out the information to be given to consumers before they sign an insurance contract. It also imposes conduct of business and transparency rules on distributors. Finally, the IDR seeks to identify and mitigate conflicts of interest, in particular in the area of commissions, and requires insurance distributors to have procedures in place to process consumer complaints promptly and fairly.

The Consumer Insurance Contracts Act 2019 (CICA) sets out requirements relating to protection, clarity, fairness, accountability, and transparency of insurance customer contracts. It applies to both life and non-life insurance. The CICA also prohibits unfair contract terms and requires insurers to handle insurance claims promptly, fairly and transparently. The CICA removed the principle of "utmost good faith" where the onus was on the consumer to disclose all facts and information which a reasonable insurer might consider to be material to the risk for which they are seeking indemnity. The pre-contractual duty of disclosure of a consumer is now confined to providing responses to questions asked by the insurer, and the consumer is not under any duty to volunteer any information over and above that required by such questions.

Box 2.1. Type of entities authorised and regulated by the Central Bank

The Central Bank regulates and supervises over 12 500 entities (see Table 2.1). This box provides a brief description of those entities which are relevant from a financial consumer protection perspective, all of which are required to obtain authorisation or registration from the Central Bank. These include:

- Credit institutions, including retail banks, are granted banking licences by the European Central Bank (ECB) under Section 9 of the Central Bank Act 1971 (as set out in Article 4 of the SSM Regulation) and are supervised by the Central Bank from a retail conduct perspective. Credit institutions are authorised to conduct a range of activities including taking deposits, lending, providing payment services and providing investment services.[2]
- Retail credit firms are defined by the Central Bank Act 1997 as firms that carry out activities including providing credit, mortgages, hire purchase/personal contract plans (PCP) and Buy Now Pay Later (BNPL) products.
- Mortgage credit intermediaries are authorised by the Central Bank under the European Union (Consumer Mortgage Credit Agreements) Regulations 2016 (CMCAR) to present or offer credit agreements to consumers, assist consumers by undertaking preparatory work or other pre-contractual administration in respect of credit agreements and conclude credit agreements with consumers on behalf of a creditor.
- Mortgage intermediaries are authorised by the Central Bank under the Consumer Credit Act 1995 to arrange for a mortgage lender to provide a consumer with a housing loan which falls outside the scope of the CMCAR (such as equity release products). Mortgage credit intermediaries may also provide these types of services.

- High-cost credit providers (which were previously known as moneylenders) are defined by the Consumer Credit Act 1995 (CCA) as a consumer credit provider offering credit agreements with an Annual Percentage Rate (APR) in excess of 23%.
- Credit servicing firms are defined by the Central Bank Act 1997 as firms holding the legal title to loans or managing loans on behalf of other entities.
- Credit unions are not-for-profits entities who take deposits from and offer loans to members of the credit union. Credit unions can also make investments. Credit unions must be registered with the Central Bank (Credit Union Act 1997). The last registration of a credit union took place in 1999.
- Payment institutions are firms offering payment services as defined in the European Union Regulations 2018 (Payment Services) Regulations 2018 (PSR), including: enabling cash to be placed on a payment account, cash withdrawals from a payment account, execution of payments transactions (via direct debit, card payment or credit transfer) (including execution of payments where funds are covered by a credit line), issue of payment instruments, acquiring of payment transactions, money remittance, payment initiation services and account information services. Payment institutions are authorised by the Central Bank under the PSR.
- Electronic money institutions can issue e-money represented by a claim on the issuer, which is issued on receipt of funds for the purpose of making payment transactions. Electronic money institutions are authorised by the Central Bank under the European Communities (Electronic Money) Regulations 2011 (EMR).
- Account information service providers provide consolidated account information in a single location on all payment accounts held by a customer. They are registered by the Central Bank under the PSR.
- Bureaux de change offer foreign currency services and they are authorised by the Central Bank under the Central Bank Act 1997.
- Non-life and life insurance companies are authorised by the Central Bank to sell specific classes of business approved in their application. These classes are set out under Schedule 1 and Schedule 2 of the European Union (Insurance and Reinsurance) Regulations 2015.
- MiFID investment firms are authorised by the Central Bank under the MiFID Regulations and, depending on their specific authorisation, can provide advice, portfolio management, and receive, transmit and execute transactions concerning financial instruments. Non-MiFID investment firms are authorised by the Central Bank under the IIA, can only provide a limited range of services and cannot passport their services to other EEA jurisdictions.
- Insurance intermediaries must be registered with the Central Bank to carry out the activity of insurance distribution, including the provision of advice in relation to insurance products.
- Investment intermediaries must be authorised by the Central Bank under the IIA if they act as a deposit agent/broker, advise on investment products or receive and transmit orders in investment instruments on behalf of consumers to other financial services providers.
- Approved professional bodies (APB) are representative of a profession such as solicitors or accountants and they are regulated under the IIA. APBs can approve its members as certified persons (i.e. persons who can undertake IIA activity subject to certain limits). The APBs must supervise and monitor certified persons.
- Debt management firms authorised under the Central Bank Act 1997 provide debt management services to consumers for remuneration including advice about the discharge of debts (in whole or in part), advice about budgeting in connection with the discharge of debts and negotiating with a person's creditors for the discharge of the person's debts (in whole or in part).

- Crowdfunding service providers are authorised by the Central Bank under the European Union (Crowdfunding) Regulations 2021 and are subject to the requirements of the EU's Crowdfunding Regulation.
- Undertakings for collective investment in transferable securities (UCITS) are a retail investment product. UCITS are authorised under the UCITS Regulations.
- Alternative Investment Funds (AIFs) are a type of collective investment where funds are raised from a number of investors with a view to investing them in accordance with a defined investment policy. They are subject to the AIFM Regulations, which transpose the AIFM Directive into Irish law, as well as the Central Bank's AIF Rulebook.
- Fund management companies are responsible for the governance, management and control of an investment fund and are authorised under the UCITS Regulations or under the AIFM Regulations.

Cross-sectoral legislation

The European Union (Key Information Documents for Packaged Retail and Insurance-based Investment Products (PRIIPs)) Regulations 2017 transposed into Irish Law the EU Regulation on key information documents for packaged retail and insurance-based products (PRIIPs Regulation). These Regulations set out standardised disclosure requirements for specified investment products including investment funds, life insurance policies with an investment element, structured investment products, structured deposits and financial instruments issued by special purpose vehicles.

The Fitness and Probity Regime (F&P Regime) was introduced under the Central Bank Reform Act 2010 and it requires firms to ensure that individuals in key controlled functions possess the necessary skills, integrity and competence to effectively perform their role and safeguard the interests of consumers. In addition, firms must seek the Central Bank's pre-approval for appointments to the most senior roles. Firms are also required to monitor the fitness and probity of individuals in key roles and to report any concerns to the Central Bank.

The recently introduced Individual Accountability Framework (IAF) comprises four key elements:

- the Senior Executive Accountability Regime (SEAR), requiring firms in-scope of the SEAR to set out clearly and fully where responsibility and decision-making lie within the firm's senior management. The SEAR became applicable to executive Pre-Approval Controlled Function (PCF) roles from 1 July 2024 and will apply to (Independent) Non-Executive Directors from 1 July 2025.
- the Common Conduct Standards, which are a set of expected standards of conduct that apply to certain individuals in regulated firms, and the Additional Conduct Standards that apply to senior executives in regulated firms since 29 December 2023,
- the enhancements to the current F&P Regime, clarifying firms' obligations to proactively certify that individuals carrying out certain specified functions are fit and proper, and
- the amendments to the Administrative Sanctions Procedure (ASP) that allows the Central Bank to take enforcement action under the ASP directly against individuals for breaches of their obligations rather than only for their participation in breaches committed by a firm.

Mechanisms to review or amend the framework

As part of its statutory objectives, the Central Bank provides analysis to support Ireland's economic policy development. This includes the Central Bank's advocacy activity for consumer protection in financial services and fair treatment of consumers at local, EU and international levels, including influencing and shaping the financial consumer protection agenda at EU level, for example via participation on the Board and in relevant Committees of European Supervisory Authorities. The Central Bank also provides technical assistance to the Department of Finance on the development of domestic legislation and transposition of EU Directives and responds to consultation papers both at EU and domestic levels.

The Central Bank can introduce standalone codes or regulations to address specific issues or risks as they are identified, and it has the authority to amend both codes and regulations it has issued. For instance, the Central Bank has issued several addenda to the existing Consumer Protection Code (Code) and has recently launched a comprehensive review of the Code as well as its transposition into regulations.

2.1.2. Codes and regulations of the Central Bank

As described above, the Central Bank can impose requirements on regulated firms to ensure that they i) act in the best interests of customers and of the integrity of the market, ii) act honestly, fairly and professionally, and iii) act with due skill, care and diligence. The Central Bank has used these powers in a number of areas, including conduct (e.g. consumer protection, management of conflicts of interest, provision of information, advertising), minimum competency requirements and dealing with customers in vulnerable circumstances. This section describes the main codes of conduct developed by the Central Bank.

In 2006 the Central Bank developed the Code, which introduces certain minimum standards of business that apply to firms providing financial services to consumers in Ireland. Since then, the Code has been amended several times. The Code applies to most regulated entities (Central Bank of Ireland, 2013[3]). However, the Code does not apply to MiFID investment firms (who are subject to investor protection requirements based on EU legislation) nor to the core savings and lending activities of credit unions or to bureaux de change. As part of the review of the Code, it is intended to bring credit unions and bureaux de change fully within its scope.

The Code aims at safeguarding consumers in their dealings with financial institutions setting out principles and rules for regulated firms regarding, *inter alia,* the provision of clear and understandable information, product suitability, fair treatment of consumers, complaints handling, and advertising of financial services. In 2021 the Central Bank updated its guidance on the Code for firms (Central Bank of Ireland, 2021[4]).

The Central Bank is currently conducting a comprehensive review of the Code. The objectives of the review are to ensure that the revised Code reflects the recent developments in Ireland's retail financial markets, enhances clarity and predictability of firms' consumer protection obligations and provides an integrated regulatory format in a more structured manner. The Central Bank published a discussion paper in October 2022 (Central Bank of Ireland, 2022[5]) and a consultation paper in March 2024 (Central Bank of Ireland, 2024[6]). As part of the Central Bank's consultation on its review of the Code, it is proposed that the Code will be re-issued as statutory regulations including Standards for Business which will build on and update the existing General Principles of the Code. The finalisation of the consultation and the enactment of these new regulations is expected for early 2025. The new regulations will aim to require, among other things, that financial services firms i) act in the best interest of customers and in the integrity of the market, ii) act honestly, fairly and professionally, and iii) act with due skills, care and diligence.

Another code of conduct of the Central Bank is the Code of Conduct on Mortgage Arrears (CCMA), which sets out measures to protect borrowers experiencing difficulties in meeting their mortgage repayments on a primary residence. The CCMA requires firms to follow a mortgage arrears resolution process when dealing with borrowers in or facing mortgage arrears. In accordance with this process, firms must provide borrowers with clear and transparent information and engage in fair and proactive communication with borrowers. They must ensure that communications are proportionate and not excessive, taking into account the borrowers' circumstances. Firms must also gather relevant information from borrowers using a specified template and examine each case on its individual merits. They must determine which options for alternative repayment arrangements offered by the firm are viable for the particular case, providing borrowers with appropriate and sustainable solutions to help them manage their mortgage arrears effectively. If an alternative repayment arrangement cannot be agreed with the borrower, the firm must inform the borrower about other options (Central Bank of Ireland, 2013[7]).

Other codes of conduct and regulations relevant for this review include: the Central Bank (Supervision and Enforcement) Act 2013 (Section 48) (Lending to Small and Medium-Sized Enterprises) Regulations 2015; Central Bank (Supervision and Enforcement) Act 2013 (Section 48(1)) (Insurance Requirements) Regulations 2022; Central Bank (Supervision and Enforcement) Act 2013 (Section 48(1)) (Investment Firms) Regulations 2023; the Code of Conduct on the Switching of Payment Accounts with Payment Service Providers (Central Bank of Ireland, 2016[8]); the Central Bank (Supervision and Enforcement) Act 2013 (Section 48 (1)) Minimum Competency Regulations 2017; the Minimum Competency Code (Central Bank of Ireland, 2017[9]) and the Central Bank (Supervision and Enforcement) Act 2013 (Section 48) (Licensed Moneylenders) Regulations 2020.The revised Code will incorporate requirements currently set out in the CCMA, Insurance Requirements and Licensed Moneylenders Regulations.

When exercising its power to make regulations under Section 48 of the Central Bank (Supervision and Enforcement) Act 2013, the Central Bank must consider the need to ensure that the requirements imposed are effective and proportionate having regard to the nature, scale and complexity of the activities of regulated financial service providers to whom the regulations will apply. Where appropriate, the Central Bank consults with interested parties during policy development in order to seek, receive, analyse and respond to feedback from all interested and affected parties on what policy response or codes, standards, regulations or guidelines would be most effective and proportionate (Central Bank of Ireland, 2024[10]). The Access to Cash Bill proposes that, before making regulations the Central Bank should also carry out and publish assessments of the costs and benefits of the proposed regulations, including consideration of the potential impacts on customers, and fair competition in financial markets.[3]

Finally, European Supervisory Authorities (ESA) guidelines and other measures are developed by ESA groups and committees to which the Central Bank contributes. The ESA issue guidelines to ensure the consistent application of EU law and are typically incorporated into the Central Bank's supervisory practices. Where these guidelines are addressed to market participants, they must make every effort to comply with them. ESA Guidelines are often issued or revised to support the application of new or revised EU legislation.

2.1.3. Guidance of the Central Bank

The Central Bank regularly provides guidance to regulated firms on how to apply the legal, regulatory and supervisory framework and to set its expectations. The tools used include i) Central Bank guidance or Q&A documents, ii) the Central Bank's Guide to Consumer Protection Risk Assessment, iii) the Central Bank's Outlook reports, including its Regulatory and Supervisory Outlook starting in 2024 and Consumer Protection Outlook Reports published up to 2023, iv) industry letters and website communications arising from thematic supervision and v) newsletters which are typically issued to consolidate material in one place (Central Bank of Ireland, 2021[11]).

In some cases, for example in the Central Bank's Consumer Protection Code Guidance, the Central Bank publishes clarifications and guidance on compliance with specific obligations. This guidance is reviewed and supplemented as compliance issues for which guidance is considered appropriate arise. Central Bank Guidance itself is typically not enforceable. However, it serves as a guide to firms on how they should approach compliance with the primary legally binding obligations set out in codes or regulations. In cases where a firm is called to account for actions or inactions (whether in a court, a tribunal/independent body, or by the Central Bank), Guidance would be an interpretative aid and can be called upon by firms.

The Central Bank's Guide to Consumer Protection Risk Assessment sets out the elements and modules of an appropriate consumer protection risk management framework and how the Central Bank carries out targeted consumer protection risk assessments.

The Central Bank's Regulatory and Supervisory Outlook (RSO) sets out the Central Bank's perspective on the key trends and risks shaping the financial sector operating landscape and the Central Bank's regulatory and supervisory priorities to support the delivery of its strategy over the next two years. The overall risk outlook and sector by sector assessment of trends, risks and vulnerabilities are provided in an integrated way taking account of all elements of the Central Bank's regulatory and supervisory mandate. In addition, the RSO includes a separate section exploring consumer risk in more detail. The "Consumer Protection Outlook" section sets out the Central Bank's assessment of the key drivers of consumer risk, and details how the Central Bank expects firms to address the drivers of the risk identified. The key drivers of consumer risk identified in the RSO published in 2024 are: poor business practices and weak business processes, ineffective disclosures to consumers, the changing operational landscape, technology-driven risks to consumer protection, and the impact of shifting business models.

Communications to industry include "Dear CEO" letters, typically following supervisory activity or a particular market development. "Dear CEO" letters are typically published on the website of the Central Bank depending on whether the findings of a particular supervisory activity may provide useful guidance to a broad cohort of firms. Letters may not be published where findings are firm specific or limited to a small number of firms (to avoid identifying particular entities) or where the matter at issue is very technical.

The Central Bank regularly issues newsletters for selected sectors, particularly those where the Central Bank regulates a large number of individual firms that have a similar business model, to consolidate in one place updates on domestic and international developments in the sectors and on the relevant activity of the Central Bank. The newsletters are published every three to six months, depending on the sector. The Central Bank publishes newsletters for intermediaries (Central Bank of Ireland, 2023[12]), insurance companies (Central Bank of Ireland, 2023[13]) and credit unions (Central Bank of Ireland, 2023[14]). The Central Bank may also publish newsletters for other sectors where there is a sufficient volume of developments to make such a publication useful. For example, the Central Bank published a newsletter for high-cost credit providers in H2 2023.

2.1.4. Licensing, authorisation, and registration

Subject to those sectors within the remit of other authorities as set out in section 1.3, the Central Bank is the competent authority in Ireland for the authorisation of financial services firms. Gatekeeping is a key part of the supervisory framework applied by the Central Bank. The Central Bank is committed to providing a clear, open and transparent authorisation process while ensuring a rigorous assessment of the applicable regulatory standards (Central Bank of Ireland, 2024[15]). While certain aspects of the authorisation process vary across sectors given the differences in business model and type and scale of services provided to end-users, the Central Bank expects each applicant to satisfy the Central Bank that it can meet the authorisation standards set out in the relevant legislation.

The Central Bank sets out authorisation standards and requirements and/or guidance where necessary to complement sectoral legislation and provides application documentation for applicant firms reflecting different sectoral requirements. These are designed to ensure that applicant firms provide the information necessary for the Central Bank to assess applications against relevant legislative and regulatory requirements. Each application for authorisation is assessed on its own merits and in the context of the sector within which it is applying. Firms are not only expected to meet the minimum authorisation standards set out in the legislation, but they are also expected to look beyond the point of authorisation and to be aware of the Central Bank's broader financial regulation expectations post-authorisation such as those set out in guidelines issued by European Supervisory Authorities and "Dear CEO" letters issued by the Central Bank.

In addition, the application process for all sectors includes the assessment of specified persons responsible for the management and direction of the firm under the Central Bank's F&P Regime.

The Central Bank publishes a regular report on its performance against regulatory service standards. This includes information about the performance of the Central Bank against the service standards relating to the authorisation of firms and investment funds, approval of prospectuses, assessment of PCF Individual Questionnaire (IQ) applications, and performance of its third-party contact management service. In the period from January to December 2023, all applicable services standards were met (Central Bank of Ireland, 2024[16]). In 2024, the Central Bank also published an Authorisation and Gatekeeping Report which provides information on the Central Bank's authorisation framework and risk appetite, its priorities and its expectations of applicant firms (Central Bank of Ireland, 2024[17]). The Report also provides insight into the operation of the F&P Regime and key challenges that it sees for firms seeking authorisation. This is the first edition of this report which will be published annually going forward.

2.1.5. Activity of the Central Bank relating to firms operating at the perimeter of the legal, regulatory and supervisory framework

To mitigate the risks to consumers arising from firms operating at the perimeter of the legal, regulatory and supervisory framework, the Central Bank undertakes several activities.

First, the Central Bank provides support for consumers to help them understand whether they are dealing with a regulated firm. It publishes warning notices naming people or firms who are providing financial services or holding themselves out to be a regulated financial services provider without having the appropriate authorisation. The Central Bank also publishes registers of authorised firms, as well as a list of the unauthorised firms that have been subject of the warning notices. Second, the Central Bank may become aware that firms are operating at the perimeter of the framework in various ways. This includes receiving protected disclosures, consumer complaints, media reports, conducting analysis of business returns and supervisory activity such as thematic reviews.

A risk posed to consumers in this area is represented by authorised firms providing unregulated services. There are certain products that can be used for financial and investment purposes that do not fall within the regulatory remit of the Central Bank. Examples include real property, certain investments, for example non-transferable loan notes and, up until recently, cryptocurrencies.[4] Where a firm authorised by the Central Bank sells unregulated products, consumers may presume that since the firm is regulated, all the services it offers are protected by standard consumer safeguards. The Central Bank may identify this risk during the authorisation process, or through the channels set out above. The Code requires firms to differentiate between regulated and unregulated services, for example by addressing these on separate sections of its website. To further mitigate this risk, the Central Bank may set expectations for firms at the time of authorisation and through the issuance of "Dear CEO" letters with a view to ensuring that disclosures as regards regulatory status of a service are effective. In addition, the review of the Code (see section 2.1.2) includes a proposal relating to "unregulated activities". The Central Bank proposes that the revised Code will introduce a requirement for firms to take appropriate steps to mitigate the risks that consumers misunderstand an activity to be regulated where this is not the case. This would require firms to clearly distinguish between the firm's regulated activities and its unregulated activities.

The Central Bank cannot ban a product from an unregulated sector, nor can it extend the regulatory perimeter to include other activities or firms. Decisions to introduce amendments to the regulatory perimeter are made by either the *Oireachtas* (Ireland's Parliament) or the European Parliament. The EU Markets in Crypto-Assets Regulation is an example of where policy makers, through primary legislation, have extended the remit of the Central Bank. The Central Bank has a key responsibility to provide advice to policy makers given its consumer protection mandate and, in this regard, can also advocate for changes where appropriate (Central Bank of Ireland, 2022[18]).

2.2. Principle 2: Role of Oversight Bodies

Principle 2 stipulates that financial oversight bodies are crucial for protecting financial consumers. They need clear responsibilities, independence and resources to be effective. These bodies must adhere to high standards, avoid conflicts of interest, and have the flexibility to adapt to new challenges. Enforcement measures should be strong, including penalties and sanctions. Collaboration among oversight authorities and international co-operation are essential for ensuring consumer protection in an evolving financial landscape.

2.2.1. Independence and accountability

The Governor of the Central Bank (Governor) is appointed by the President of Ireland on the advice of the Government. The Governor holds office for seven years and may be reappointed for one additional period of seven years. There are several mechanisms to ensure the independence of the Governor and the Deputy Governors. The procedures for their appointment are transparent and set out in the Central Bank Act 1942. Moreover, there are limited circumstances in which the Governor could cease to hold office, and these are set out in the Central Bank Act 1942.

The Central Bank Reform Act 2010 established the Central Bank Commission (Commission), which comprises the Governor, the Deputy Governors, the Secretary General of the Department of Finance and six members appointed by the Minister of Finance. The objectives of the Commission are to manage and control the activities of the Central Bank, to ensure that the Central Bank's financial regulation and supervisory functions are co-ordinated and integrated, and to ensure that the statutory powers and functions of the Central Bank are properly exercised and discharged (Central Bank of Ireland, 2024[19]).

The Central Bank is accountable to the *Oireachtas*. The Central Bank Act 1942 requires the Central Bank to publish a Strategic Plan every three years, and a statement related to the performance of the Central Bank before 30 April each year. The Central Bank Act 1942 also states that the *Oireachtas* can require the Central Bank officials to provide evidence to inquiries and Central Bank officials appear regularly before parliamentary committees. The Central Bank is also subject to Freedom of Information requirements and is required to respond to written questions submitted to Ministers by Members of the *Dáil Éireann* (the Lower House of Ireland's Parliament). The Central Bank responded to 239 parliamentary queries in 2022 and 211 in 2023, half of which related directly to consumer protection topics.

Finally, the Central Bank Act 1942 requires the Central Bank to make arrangements for an international peer review of the performance of its regulatory functions at least every four years.

2.2.2. Mandate of the Central Bank

The mandate of the Central Bank covers the maintenance of price and financial stability through monetary policy and other measures, the soundness of individual firms through prudential supervision, and the protection of consumers and investors through a mix of rules, supervision and enforcement. Regarding the Central Bank's responsibilities relating to consumer protection, the Central Bank Act 1942 sets out the objectives of the Central Bank which include "*proper and effective regulation of financial service providers and markets, while ensuring that the best interests of consumers of financial services are protected*".

2.2.3. Resources and capabilities

The Central Bank is of the view that it has adequate resources (i.e. financial and human resources) and capabilities (i.e. the technical skills of staff and/or the equipment that staff require to fulfil their role) to effectively carry out its financial consumer protection supervisory functions for its current statutory responsibilities. The Central Bank's Strategy acknowledges the need to invest in new skills and capabilities, become more agile, and look for continuous improvement in its ways of working to meet the challenges of an evolving financial system. Regarding resources, the Central Bank is committed to seeking efficiencies and to prioritising in line with its risk-based approach to supervision. While each new mandate received by a supervisory authority needs to be considered to assess whether additional resources are required, in some cases the Central Bank has assumed new responsibilities such as the authorisation and supervision of Buy Now Pay Later (BNPL) services providers and Personal Contract Plan (PCP) services providers without increasing its headcount, which totalled 2 234 FTEs as of 31 December 2023 (Central Bank of Ireland, 2024[20]).

Regarding capabilities, the Central Bank provides training programmes to address learning needs of its employees including both bespoke programmes (such as One Bank Foundation, One Bank Curriculum and One Bank Leadership Training) as well as supporting employees to undertake further academic and professional qualifications. The Learning and Development function of the Central Bank implemented a Learning and Development Strategy for the period 2023-2026. The goals of the Learning and Development Strategy (L&D Strategy) include developing stronger alignment between learning and development and business goals and building future skills and capabilities. As part of the L&D Strategy, the Central Bank has developed a Technical Training Academy with training content aligned to business needs inclusive of training for supervisors.

The Central Bank's strategy calls out the need for investment in new skills and capabilities and the importance of ensuring its employees have the tools to use data effectively. The Central Bank's data strategy aims to increase the data competency of the organisation, including investing in broadening and deepening the Central Bank's data capabilities. The data strategy also seeks to strengthen data and analytical capabilities and capacity through increased collaboration across the Central Bank and alignment on data initiatives.

2.2.4. Risks assessment and prioritisation

The responsibility to implement the Central Bank's supervisory mandate falls under the Supervisory Risk Committee (SRC). The objectives of the SRC are to develop and maintain the Central Bank's supervisory strategy, approach and risk-based framework, to oversee the implementation of the supervisory strategy, to monitor and analyse supervisory risks and determine the Central Bank's response, to lead the Central Bank's supervision, including deciding on supervisory policies, practices and activities and ensure a "One Bank" approach to supervision. The SRC is also responsible for overseeing international peer reviews of the performance of Central Bank's regulatory functions.

The Central Bank applies a risk-based supervisory approach and allocates resources and makes interventions based on an assessment of the level of risk posed by individual institutions or sectors within the financial system. To assess and address retail conduct risks, the Central Bank adopts a Retail Conduct Supervisory Framework (RCSF), which includes a Sectoral Supervision Model and a Firm-Specific Model, each conducted over a multi-year supervisory cycle. The next paragraphs provide details on both models.

The Sectoral Supervision Model identifies the key retail conduct risks in each sector. The key stages of the Sectoral Supervision Model are:

- an annual Sectoral Risk Assessment (SRA), which identifies the current and emerging retail conduct risks and sources of potential consumer harm. This process draws on supervisory, policy and behavioural economics expertise within the Central Bank; on knowledge gained from ongoing supervisory interactions with firms and through stakeholder engagement activities (described in section 2.2.11); on risk identification activities (described in section 2.2.6), trigger-based reporting (described in section 2.2.9) and consumer research (described in sections 2.7.3 and 2.8.3); and on Central Bank macro-economic reports, international European Supervisory Authorities (ESAs) reports, and reports on topical issues such as frauds and scams, climate change and cyber-crime. Risks identified during workshops are scored and ranked based on impact and probability.

- risk treatments are developed for each identified retail conduct risk. The particular risk treatment will depend on what is most appropriate to either further assess or address the particular retail conduct risk. Treatments can range from a specific supervisory intervention, such as carrying out a thematic review; an industry communication; a policy intervention; undertaking further research; or issuing a consumer warning.
- the development of a multi-year Sectoral Strategy, which sets out sectoral priorities, desired outcomes and high-level activities to address sectoral risks. There are a number of inputs into Sectoral Strategies including the risks identified through the SRA process and their associated risk treatments; the cross-sectoral risks; the Central Bank's strategic priorities; the EU and European Supervisory Authorities priorities; the advice from the Central Bank's Consumer Advisory Group; and the domestic priorities.
- the development and implementation of a Supervisory Engagement Plan to set out an operational plan of work aligned with the Sectoral Strategy.
- a review of the Sectoral Strategy by a Sector Strategy Governance Panel (SSGP), at least once every three years. The SSGP incorporates perspectives from various areas of the Central Bank's remit (supervisory, policy and research).
- the publication of the Regulatory and Supervisory Outlook Report including the outputs of the SRA (Central Bank of Ireland, 2024[1]).

The Firm-Specific Model applies to a very small number of the most impactful firms, with impact being assessed based on size (i.e. number of customers) and product score (which reflects the relative importance of the product to consumers).

The Central Bank assesses retail conduct risks under the Firm-Specific Model across six key drivers: Business Model and Strategy, Governance and Controls, Product Development, Sales/Transactions Process, Post-sales Handling and People and Culture. To assess the firm-specific risks relating to Business Model and Strategy, the Central Bank seeks to understand:

- the business environment in which the firm operates,
- risks to consumers posed by the firm's business model and strategy,
- whether the business environment may result in commercial (or other) pressures to make decisions that could ultimately be detrimental for customers.

To assess the firm-specific risks relating to the remaining five risk drivers, the Central Bank uses the Consumer Protection Risk Assessment (CPRA) model. For each of the five drivers, the Guide to CPRA provides examples of positive practices to manage risks to consumers (Central Bank of Ireland, 2017[21]). The outcome of the risk assessments is considered by a Risk Governance Panel (RGP), which comprises supervisors and senior management from different areas of the Central Bank. The RGP has the objective to ensure that a holistic approach has been used and that views from across the Central Bank have been taken into account.

The RCSF also acknowledges that trigger events will occur outside of planned supervisory engagements, which the Central Bank may become aware of through trigger-based reporting from firms (as described in section 2.2.9) or through protected disclosures (as described in section 2.2.10), public contacts, social media monitoring or media queries. Where the risk is more immediate, the RCSF allows the Central Bank to re-focus supervisory resources on the risk that has materialised. Where the event triggers a less urgent risk, action may be built into the supervisory strategy for the following cycle.

The Central Bank has published an explanation of how the Central Bank's risk prioritisation process is used to identify the risks set out in the Central Bank Outlook reports (Central Bank of Ireland, 2022[22]).

The Central Bank also deploys a risk-based approach in authorising and supervising investment funds and fund management companies. In the case of investment funds which may be marketed to retail investors, such as UCITS, the Central Bank reviews each application for authorisation focusing on the areas of higher risk such as investment objective, policies and strategy, fees and expenses, examining compliance with applicable legislative requirements and considering the appropriateness of an asset class for the end consumer. From a supervisory perspective, the Central Bank may probe to ensure that the investment structure is fully understood by the fund management company and is subject to robust oversight. The Central Bank may also seek to determine whether a particular structure is appropriate for retail investors by considering, for example, investor types that are targeted by the distribution strategy.

The Central Bank's Retail Conduct Supervisory Framework does not operate in isolation. The Central Bank supervises firms from a i) prudential; ii) retail conduct; iii) wholesale conduct; and iv) anti-money laundering and counter terrorist financing perspective. As such, the Central Bank applies a number of supervisory frameworks to assess the risks that might arise under any and all of these four lenses. Regarding prudential risk, the Central Bank uses a prudential risk framework that categorises firms into different risk categories based on the probability and potential impact of the risk: High impact, Medium-High impact, Medium-Low impact, and Low impact. In discharging its prudential supervisory functions, the Central Bank considers a firm's business model, governance, risk management and operational capabilities and resilience, which can implicitly protect consumers from harm that can be caused by failure in any of these areas.

In line with its Strategy, the Central Bank is transforming its approach to regulation and supervision. While continuing to be a risk-based framework, the Central Bank's supervisory framework will evolve to deliver a more integrated approach to supervision, across its overall mandate. This aims to position the Central Bank to continue to meet its objectives and ensure consumers of financial services are protected in a changing and increasingly complex and interconnected financial landscape. The integrated, risk-based supervisory approach incorporates the key aspects of the Retail Conduct Supervisory Framework outlined above. The new supervisory approach will be applied in an integrated way, including for example holistic risk identification for sectors and firms.

2.2.5. Data policies, procedures and capabilities

The Central Bank regularly uses data in the exercise of its financial consumer protection supervisory functions. The Central Bank's data policies, procedures and capabilities include data collection, analysis, sharing data across the organisation as well as publication of financial statistics. The next paragraphs describe each of these elements. Policies relating to the protection of personal data and information security policy are described in section 2.11.

The Central Bank regularly collects data from firms via regulatory returns that vary depending on the characteristics of the sector. Regular data returns are submitted via a Portal. The Central Bank has several mechanisms to engage with firms in respect of the submitted returns and analytical tools with which to make use of the data. For example, Central Bank employees can engage with firms in respect to the submitted returns using Unity, the internal interface of the Portal that can analyse the returns using an off-the-shelf data visualisation tool, and OMNI, an analytics application which the Central Bank uses for prudential data. In relation to the funds sector, the Central Bank uses tools to conduct analysis on structured and unstructured data (such as text mining or topic modelling). The Central Bank also collects data from firms on an ad-hoc basis for various purposes, such as thematic supervisory activity or firm-specific work following, for example, a breach or error report, a protected disclosure, or a public contact which, on review, indicates a potential systemic issue.

As the main compiler of Irish financial statistics, the Central Bank also regularly publishes data and commentary on credit and deposit developments, interest rates, investment funds and securities. Statistical data collections also inform the work on consumer protection conducted by the Central Bank and support market analysis. Examples of such collections include mortgage arrears data which provides quarterly updates on volumes and values of mortgages in arrears, restructured mortgages and repossessed properties for both residential and buy-to-let properties. This dataset is used to monitor delinquency and restructuring trends in the market and informs the Central Bank's consumer protection supervision, for example in the context of its work on mortgage arrears described in section 2.3.3 below.

The Central Bank operates the Central Credit Register (CCR) under the Credit Reporting Act 2013. The CCR is a mandatory, comprehensive database that stores personal and credit information on loans and credit applications and provides credit reports to borrowers and lenders. The CCR started collecting data in July 2017, and began issuing credit reports in March 2018. The Central Bank has begun to use the data contained in the CCR to support its assessment of the risks facing consumers in the credit and lending sectors (see, for example, (Gaffney and Lyons, 2024[23])), as well as to inform its statistical publications.

A third-party review of the Central Bank's consumer protection sectoral risk assessment process in 2019, and an internal gap analysis of the consumer protection framework, both identified the need to further increase the Central Bank's use of structured data and further develop a more structured approach to data and analytics. This is an area of financial supervision where the development of quantitative metrics can be more challenging, and innovation is required on how to best monitor consumer and market developments.

This objective is aligned with the Central Bank's overall strategy which aims to change how it uses data and analytics to drive effectiveness. The strategy identified that key changes were required in how the Central Bank works with data including cross-Bank collaboration, analytical skills, capacity and technology. The Central Bank has undertaken a number of activities to address this. This includes establishing new specialist competency areas (e.g. data science) which operate in a decentralised way across the organisation. The Central Bank has also put in place a new cross-Bank Data Board to provide overall strategic direction on data for the Central Bank, and improve overall data maturity across the organisation. The Central Bank is also working on a new cloud based advanced analytics platform which supports enhanced use of data analytics. A research exchange has also been set up to move beyond conventional analytical techniques and datasets to help answer new questions or approach existing research topics in a new way (Central Bank of Ireland, 2024[24]).

Given the speed of development in the data landscape, the Central Bank continues to develop the appropriate skills and capability to take advantage of new emerging opportunities and tools to use data to support effective consumer protection. Some of the current and future intended focus of this enhanced work to support the Central Bank's financial consumer protection objectives includes:

- additions and enhancements to the data it currently receives (for example via social media monitoring or via returns received from firms); and
- enhanced use of existing data including through:
    - a robust data governance framework to ensure data is accessible and usable across relevant aspects of its mandate;
    - new tools/platforms to enable the use of advanced analytics including empowering greater use of data to support decision making and overall effectiveness; and
    - ensuring that relevant supervisory teams have the capabilities to use the data and tools available to them. For example, the Central Bank is developing a connected internal system that provides supervisors with access to required supervisory data via a single tool.

The intended outcome is that the Central Bank will move towards a more structured, data driven and data informed approach to retail conduct risk identification.

2.2.6. Monitoring markets and firms

The Central Bank regulates and supervises over 12 500 entities across financial markets. Table 2.1 provides information on the firms for which Ireland is the home Member State or that have a branch in Ireland, as of 31 December 2023. It does not include the firms that are passporting into Ireland on a Freedom of Services basis.

Table 2.1. Type and number of entities regulated by the Central Bank

Type of firm	Number of authorised firms
Credit Institutions	52
Life Insurance Companies	41
Non-Life Insurance Companies	94
Reinsurance Companies	61
Investment Firms	102
Fund Service Providers	204
Retail Intermediaries	2 637
Collective Investment Funds	8 942
Credit Unions	191
Money Transmitters and Bureaux de Change	7
High-Cost Credit Providers	29
Regulated Market/Market Operator	1
Moneybrokers	5
Retail Credit Firms & Transitional Retail Credit Firms	42
Payment Institutions	24
Debt Management Firms	36
Crowdfunding Service Providers	5
Electronic Money Institutions	28
Credit Servicing Firms & Transitional Credit Servicing Firms	21
Account Information Service Providers	4
Total	12 563

Source: Central Bank of Ireland (2024[20]), Annual Report 2023 and Annual Performance Statement 2023-2024, https://www.centralbank.ie/news/article/blog-the-central-banks-2023-annual-report-performance-statement

To monitor these markets and the activities of these firms, the Central Bank conducts a number of activities. These include monitoring complaints data, carrying out on-site inspections, analysing business returns from firms, engaging with stakeholders, surveying consumers, monitoring social media and conducting mystery shopping exercises. This section describes each of these activities. The Central Bank:

- uses consumer complaints data to monitor markets as an input to the annual SRA, to identify potential issues with specific firms and as an input into the selection of firms for the Central Bank's thematic supervisory activity. Section 2.2.7 provides more information on thematic supervision and section 2.12.4 for more information on use of complaints data.
- conducts on-site inspections as part of its thematic supervision work (see section 2.2.7).
- analyses returns submitted by firms (see section 2.2.5).
- engages with industry, consumer representatives, other public stakeholders and other authorities including at domestic, EU and international levels (see section 2.2.11).
- takes account of information contained in protected disclosures (as described in section 2.2.10) and in queries from the public (as described in section 2.2.11).

- uses a third-party supplier to monitor publicly available social media and online platforms. This information is used by the Central Bank to identify trends on issues and complaints regarding financial services and products. This primarily informs the Central Bank's SRA process and thematic supervision work and inspections. The Central Bank is currently revising its social media monitoring strategy to encompass more sophisticated, wide-ranging and automated functionality.
- monitors regulated firms' advertising through thematic supervisory activities to scrutinise content, claims and disclosures to assess compliance with regulatory requirements. For example, in 2023, the Central Bank participated in ESMA's common supervisory action on the application of MiFID II disclosure rules with regard to marketing and advertising across the European Union. The Central Bank communicated the results of this work in October 2024 (Central Bank of Ireland, 2023[25]). As part of its revised social media monitoring strategy, the Central Bank intends to also include a broader focus on advertising monitoring.
- conducts a market monitoring exercise within the Central Bank twice a year to collate and share information across the Central Bank's mandate. This includes a survey to various Central Bank teams collecting information on emerging products and related risks to consumers, risks to market integrity and risks to financial stability.
- from a market abuse perspective, conducts re-active work to monitor market prices and suspicious transactions based on the "suspicious transaction order reports" received from trading venues and professionals arranging or executing transactions. From 2024, the Central Bank will also conduct pro-active work to scrutinise order books and executions to detect market abuse.

Finally, the Central Bank has recently resumed the use of mystery shopping, publishing a Consumer Research Bulletin in October 2024 to explain how mystery shopping has provided an enhanced understanding of how investors engage with advertising and marketing materials of investment firms, informing the Central Bank's supervisory work (Central Bank of Ireland, 2024[26]).

2.2.7. Thematic supervision

The Central Bank regularly undertakes thematic supervision activities as part of its Supervisory Engagement Plans to mitigate the risks identified in the SRA. Thematic supervision activities involve conducting in-depth assessments of specific risks or themes across a group of regulated entities within an industry sector or across sectors and may focus on a particular product, practice, delivery channel or activity. The objective is typically to assess whether firms are complying with the relevant regulations, implementing guidance or addressing a particular risk. Thematic supervisory activity can also sometimes identify an industry-wide issue which may require introduction or amendment of legislation or regulation to secure appropriate change.

The following list is a sample of the thematic supervisory work (including, but not limited to thematic reviews) undertaken by the Central Bank and published in 2023. This report will refer to these and other activities of the Central Bank as appropriate:

- expectations for payment and e-money institutions in relation to safeguarding, business model and strategic risk, and governance, risk management, conduct and culture following thematic supervisory engagements on these topics (January 2023) (Central Bank of Ireland, 2023[27]);
- review of the costs and fees charged by UCITS (investment funds) (March 2023) (Central Bank of Ireland, 2023[28]);
- targeted reviews on control frameworks and risk appetite statements in MiFID investment firms (March 2023) (Central Bank of Ireland, 2023[29]);
- update on the Central Bank's work to protect consumers in a changing economic landscape (April 2023) (Central Bank of Ireland, 2023[30]);

- thematic inspection of product oversight and governance in non-life insurance undertakings (June 2023) (Central Bank of Ireland, 2023[31]);
- thematic review on the ongoing suitability of long-term life assurance products (August 2023) (Central Bank of Ireland, 2023[32]);
- review of differential pricing regulations in the private car and home insurance markets (December 2023) (Central Bank of Ireland, 2021[33]);
- thematic review of MiFID investment firms' application of the costs and charges disclosure requirements in MiFID (December 2023) (Central Bank of Ireland, 2023[25]);
- review of asset valuation in the investment fund sector (December 2023) (Central Bank of Ireland, 2023[34]).

The key steps of thematic reviews include:

- Scoping. The scoping of the thematic review sets out the objectives, methodology, project planning, the analysis related to risks, assumptions, issues and dependencies (RAID) and the internal and external stakeholder engagement plan.
- Firm selection. The decision about which firms to include in the review can be based on a variety of factors including market share (e.g. number of (retail) consumers), impact score, information from business returns including complaints data, compliance history of the firm, market intelligence from supervisors, consumers, members of the public or media reports and the search for appropriate geographic representation.
- Conducting the review. The Central Bank notifies selected firms at the beginning of the review, setting out the documentation to be provided in advance of the inspection and during the on-site inspection, which may include a sample of customer files as well as the firm's written processes and procedures. In addition to reviewing this documentation, members of the supervisory team typically carry out on-site inspections at the firms' premises, holding meetings and having walkthroughs with relevant firm personnel. Following on-site inspections, key findings are included in a 'Firm Specific Report' that sets out the proposed supervisory findings and proposed actions.
- Thematic Risk Governance Panel (RGP). The outcome of thematic reviews are typically reviewed by a thematic Risk Governance Panel (RGP), which is composed of senior management from the supervising Divisions and other Directorates and subject matter experts. The objective of the RGP is to gather views and expertise from different areas of the Central Bank and to help calibrate the judgements of the supervisory team. Narrowly focused thematic reviews may not have an RGP but rather are subject to governance arrangements within the relevant Directorate.
- Conclusions of the review. The Central Bank notifies firms included in the review of the outcomes, which may include good and bad practices identified across the industry as well as any proposed Risk Mitigation Programme or enforcement actions regarding the particular firm. The Central Bank also publishes a "Dear CEO" letter as appropriate, which sets out the outcomes that are relevant to the industry as a whole.
- Follow up actions. The Central Bank follows up to ensure that Risk Mitigation Programmes are addressed and may also use subsequent thematic reviews to assess whether their desired outcome has been achieved.

The Central Bank regularly communicates its thematic supervision priorities to external stakeholders. For example, the Central Bank's Regulatory and Supervisory Outlook includes the key drivers of consumer risk identified during the SRA process as well as the expected work of the Central Bank to address those drivers.

The Central Bank also communicates the outcomes of its thematic supervision activities. They are communicated to the firms within the scope of the review using "post-inspection" letters, and publicly using

"Dear CEO" letters published on the website of the Central Bank, setting out key findings and expectations for regulated firms. The Central Bank also uses other established channels of communication, such as newsletters, to emphasise and reiterate findings and expectations for the industry.

2.2.8. Supervisory tools and enforcement powers

The Central Bank has a number of supervisory tools and enforcement powers available to require firms to undertake certain activities (such as, for example, audits, remediation programmes, payment of compensation and/or restitution, issue of public notices or provision of information to the Central Bank). Following a statutory investigation, the Central Bank may impose administrative fines and/ or alternative sanctions (such as caution or reprimand, a direction to refund or withhold all or part of an amount of money charged or paid, prohibiting individuals from performing controlled functions), revoke or suspend a firm's license, authorisation or registration, issue warnings and public notices about unauthorised firms, and apply for criminal prosecution.

The Central Bank takes a targeted and proportionate approach to the use of its enforcement powers. The Central Bank considers how its regulatory objectives are best achieved, following supervisory engagements and guidance and the use of supervisory tools. This means that the Central Bank takes enforcement action only in cases where it believes that such significant action is merited, following a consideration of all the facts of the case, including the seriousness of the suspected breach, the harm or potential harm involved to consumers or investors or financial stability together with its other supervisory priorities, and the particular context of the specific financial services sector.

Supervisory tools

In terms of supervisory tools, the Central Bank often imposes Risk Mitigation Programmes (RMPs) to require firms to undertake certain activities. RMPs set out the risks identified, the actions required to be undertaken by the firm, a timeframe and the desired outcomes.

For example, in 2020 the Central Bank carried out an exercise to consider any risks arising to consumers of financial products at the beginning of the COVID-19 pandemic. The Central Bank identified business interruption as a potential risk to consumers. While not all business interruption insurance policies provided cover in the circumstances, others did. The Central Bank issued an RMP to firms providing business interruption insurance with policy wordings that were determined to be responsive to the outbreak of COVID-19 in Ireland and where firms had not proactively accepted valid claims early in the process. RMPs included an expectation that these firms identify and contact potentially affected policyholders, assist policyholders in making a claim, were operationally ready to deal with claims and had adequate governance and oversight of the process (Central Bank of Ireland, 2020[35]).

If a firm does not respond to supervisory intervention within a reasonable period of time, the Central Bank may use statutory powers to direct it to take specific action to bring its conduct into compliance with the required regulatory standards. Should the firm fail to comply with a statutory direction or other supervisory measure, or if a firm is identified as an outlier following a thematic review, then enforcement action may be considered.

Product interventions

The Central Bank's power to ban financial products or services, or specific features of such products or services is limited to insurance-based investment products and investment products (MiFIR and the PRIIPs Regulation are the source of these powers, and they also allow for the prohibition of types of financial activities or practices). In terms of exercising these powers, the Central Bank has used its powers under MiFIR to ban the sale of binary options to retail investors and has restricted the sale of contracts for difference. In some instances, the Central Bank has observed in follow-up reviews to its supervisory activities changes in firms' product offerings without the exercise of the power to prohibit a product. For example, in 2023 the Central Bank conducted analysis subsequent to its Structured Retail Products Review (Central Bank of Ireland, 2022[36]) and observed that the firms in the sample had removed a particularly complex feature from their product offerings.

The Central Bank can also make regulations for the proper and effective regulation of regulated financial services providers which could include restrictions or prohibitions on certain financial activities or practices. For example, it has banned price walking in the home and motor insurance markets. Price walking in this context refers to a practice where a customer is charged a higher premium the longer they remain with an insurance provider and for no reason other than staying with the same provider. As a result of the ban on price walking, insurance providers cannot charge retail consumers who are on their second or subsequent renewal a premium higher than they would have charged them if they were a year one renewal consumer at that point in time (Central Bank of Ireland, 2021[33]).

Sanctions

In 2022, the Central Bank concluded 8 Administrative Sanction Procedures (ASP), imposed 1 individual sanction under the securities markets assessor regime, published 112 warning notices in respect to unauthorised firms (which represents a 24% increase compared to 2021), refused the pre-approval of 3 individuals on Fitness and Probity grounds, issued 2 prohibition notices and imposed over EUR 213 million in fines, which was the highest amount imposed in a single year (Central Bank of Ireland, 2023[37]).

Table 2.2 shows the number of outcomes under the administrative sanction procedures, the securities markets assessor regime, prohibitions under the Fitness and Probity Regime (F&P Regime), involuntary revocations of authorisation and the warning notices issued regarding unauthorised firms in 2021, 2022 and 2023.

Table 2.2. Number of enforcement actions concluded by the Central Bank in 2021, 2022 and 2023

	2021	2022	2023
Number of outcomes under the administrative sanctions procedures and Assessor Regime and prohibitions under the Fitness and Probity regime and involuntary revocations of authorisation.	9	11	4
Warning Notices regarding unauthorised providers	90	112	136

Source: Central Bank's response to the OECD questionnaire

The Central Bank typically publishes the outcome of its enforcement actions to external stakeholders where permitted in accordance with its statutory powers (Central Bank of Ireland, 2024[38]). This is done by publishing public notices on the Central Bank website (including ASP, prohibition notices and revocations notices) as well as publishing aggregate statistics on the number of actions and the total fines in the Central Bank's annual report. While enforcement priorities are not published, supervisory priorities set on an annual basis may inform enforcement priorities.

Redress and restitution

As described in section 2.12, the Financial Services and Pensions Ombudsman (FSPO) has the statutory function of resolving complaints about the conduct of regulated financial service providers and pension providers. However, the Central Bank also has powers to require firms to compensate customers in the form of:

- Redress. Since 2013 the Central Bank has the power to direct a regulated firm to make redress to customers in those circumstances where the Central Bank considers that defaults by the regulated firm (such as charging a customer an amount that the firm is not entitled to charge, or providing a service that the customer did not agree to receive, or providing the customer with inaccurate information which influences the customer in making a decision about any financial service, or providing a customer with a financial service which was not suitable for the customer at the time it was provided, or a failure of the firm's systems and controls) have been widespread and that, as a result of those defaults, the customers have been harmed; and

- Restitution. Where a regulated firm has been convicted of an offense or has been subject of an administrative sanction, and the regulated firm was unjustly enriched or more than one other person suffered a loss, the Central Bank can apply to the High Court for an order requiring the regulated firm to pay amounts to the Central Bank for distribution to persons indicated in the court order.

2.2.9. Trigger-based reporting requirements

There are a number of different triggers requiring regulated entities or key individuals within a regulated entity to make a report to the Central Bank.

Section 38 (2) of the Central Bank (Supervision and Enforcement) Act 2013 requires that, subject to certain exceptions, individuals in key positions within a regulated firm, referred to in the legislation as pre-approval-controlled functions (PCFs), must disclose information relating to breaches of financial services legislation to the Central Bank, where that individual believes the disclosure will be of material assistance to the Central Bank.

In addition to specific regulatory requirements placed on firms in some sectors to report breaches to the Central Bank, the Central Bank expects firms to notify it of significant breaches of legislation and corrective measures that firms propose to take, particularly when remediating consumers.

The Code provides that where an error affecting consumers has not been fully resolved within 40 business days of its discovery, the firm must inform the Central Bank within five business days of that deadline. The term "error" is not defined in the Code but would include any error or oversight that would need to be resolved to ensure that consumers receive the full, proper and expected service under their engagement with the firm. The Code requires firms to resolve all errors speedily and no later than six months after the date the error was first discovered. The current timescales for reporting to the Central Bank allow firms the opportunity to resolve errors within 40 business days while errors that take longer to address, and that may be more complex in nature, must be reported to the Central Bank. The Central Bank recently consulted on enhancing firms' governance obligations in respect of errors, while also modifying the requirement to report them to focus on the most significant ones.

Some reporting requirements are more tailored to specific sectors. For example,

- investment firms holding client assets are required to inform the Central Bank of all breaches of the Central Bank's Client Asset Requirements
- payment services providers (including credit institutions, payment and e-money institutions) must report major operational or security incidents to the Central Bank without undue delay
- investment firms and fund management companies must notify the Central Bank when they become aware of breaches of relevant legislation.

All breach and error reports received are reviewed and, if necessary, investigated by the Central Bank. The objectives of investigations into breach and error reports are to ensure that steps are taken to mitigate risks to consumers and to identify and prioritise cases that may cause harm to consumers or where firms have breached their regulatory obligations. For each report, an initial assessment is carried out with a view to determining the complexity, severity, consumer detriment and likelihood of the issue being widespread, which determines priority and the supervisory engagement. For issues considered to be medium or lower priority, the Central Bank may request additional information from the reporting firm. The report might be closed without any further supervisory action depending on the information provided and changes proposed by the firm. In other cases, the Central Bank may carry out further investigations and/or issue an RMP. Errors and breaches impacting consumers can enter the public domain and attract media attention, which may drive the extent of supervisory engagement, resulting in medium or low priority issues attracting substantial supervisory engagement.

While the Central Bank does not publish statistics about breach and error reporting, the information contained in breach and error reports feeds into the Central Bank's annual sectoral risk assessment process, the results of which are reflected in the Central Bank's Regulatory and Supervisory Outlook Report, including in the description of the key drivers of risks to consumers.

The Central Bank expects firms to be aware of their reporting obligations under applicable regulatory regimes, but also reminds them of their obligations as regards breach and error reporting on its website and via "Dear CEO" letters, and provides guidance and template notification forms so that it is clear to firms what information must be provided.

2.2.10. Protected disclosures (or whistleblowing)

The Central Bank is a prescribed person for the purpose of receiving protected disclosures under the Protected Disclosures Act 2014. In addition, the Central Bank is designated to receive protected disclosures under Part 5 of the Central Bank (Supervision and Enforcement) Act 2013. This means that a protected disclosure may be made to the Central Bank where i) a worker makes a disclosure which they believe is substantially true and which they have obtained in a work-related context, or ii) any person in good faith makes a disclosure, and they have reasonable grounds for believing that the disclosure will show that there has been, is being or is likely to be a breach of, or an offence under, financial services legislation or the concealment or destruction of evidence relating to such an offence or breach.

The Central Bank's Protected Disclosures Desk, a dedicated team within the Central Bank, received 224 protected disclosures in 2023, 245 in 2022, and 231 in 2021 (Central Bank of Ireland, 2023[37]). All protected disclosures are investigated.

In line with legislative requirements, the Central Bank reports yearly on the protected disclosures it has received (Central Bank of Ireland, 2024[20]). While the publication does not include detailed information on, for example, the breakdown of the protected disclosures by sector or issue, the Central Bank has communicated the top three overarching themes of investigations into protected disclosures completed in 2023. The top three overarching themes were:

- fraud and other criminal offences
- governance
- fitness and probity

Not every investigation leads to a supervisory outcome. There are a variety of reasons for this but most often this is because the information in the protected disclosure was inaccurate or there was a lack of evidence to support the issues raised, or the issues raised did not fall within the remit of the Central Bank.

2.2.11. Engagement with stakeholders

The Central Bank regularly engages with stakeholders. In 2021 the Central Bank undertook a consultation to seek views on its stakeholder engagement activity (Central Bank of Ireland, 2021[39]). The key deliverables of the consultation paper include the establishment of several initiatives to enhance engagement with a wide range of stakeholders. These initiatives include the Financial Industry Forum, the

Civil Society Roundtables and the Financial System Conference (see below for a description of these initiatives), and the creation of the Stakeholder Engagement Team within the Central Bank.

Following the consultation, the Central Bank published its 2022-24 Strategy (Strategy) (Central Bank of Ireland, 2021[40]). One of the four key themes of the Strategy is "Open and Engaged" and it highlights the importance of listening to stakeholders, building dialogue, and fostering a wider understanding of the role of the Central Bank to build trust in the financial system.

Consistent with its Strategy, the Central Bank engages with a number of stakeholders both on a regular and an ad-hoc basis. Central Bank's stakeholders can be grouped into several categories: members of the public and consumers of financial services, including consumer representatives; the government and public representatives including other Irish authorities that play a role in financial consumer protection; regulated entities and industry bodies; other EU and international policy institutions and peers; and media and public commentators. The next paragraphs provide details on the engagement of the Central Bank with each of these groups separately. The introduction of the Financial System Conference in 2022 provided an opportunity to bring together all the Central Bank's stakeholders to discuss issues shaping the financial system. In 2023, more than 800 people joined the event in-person and online.

Engagement with consumer representatives and the public

The Central Bank conducts regular engagement activities with a range of consumer representatives. Activities include regular meetings with the Consumer Advisory Group, roundtables with civil society organisations, an annual stakeholder engagement plan and regular engagement about risk drivers identified in the Central Bank's Outlook Reports and engagement on public consultations. The next paragraphs describe these activities.

The Consumer Advisory Group (CAG) is a Central Bank appointed group of individuals with expertise on matters including financial regulation, consumer finance, consumer advocacy and behavioural economics. Established by the Central Bank Reform Act 2010, the role of the CAG is to advise the Central Bank on the performance of its functions and the exercise of its powers in relation to consumers of financial services, including on the effects of the Central Bank's Strategic Plans on consumers of financial services, and on the initiatives aimed at further enhancing the protection of consumers of financial services. The CAG also advises, at the request of the Central Bank, on consultation papers or other materials prepared by the Central Bank. Members of the CAG are appointed by the Central Bank Commission, their appointment lasts three years, and they are eligible for re-appointment.

Following its consultation paper on enhancing engagement with stakeholders, the Central Bank increased the membership of CAG, with a view to enhancing capacity and maintaining its strong insights and experience on consumer needs and consumer risks.

Civil Society Roundtables are meetings between the Central Bank's senior officers and a range of charitable and civil society organisations that provide support to different consumer groups.[5] Civil Society Roundtables are organised two to three times a year and agendas are based on topical areas and developed in consultation with members of the groups (Central Bank of Ireland, 2024[41]). In addition, targeted roundtables are held with representatives from civil society where necessary to inform key policy areas such as the Review of the Code.

Following its consultation paper on enhancing engagement with stakeholders, the Central Bank undertook an analysis of the membership of the Civil Society Roundtable and has sought to address any gaps in civil society representation by inviting additional representatives, with a particular focus on ensuring that the breadth of society is represented. This process continues and potential new members are, where possible, identified and then invited to engage in the group.

In addition, the Central Bank also develops an annual stakeholder engagement plan focussed on consumer protection risk and priorities. As part of this plan, in 2023 the financial consumer protection supervisory team participated in over 30 stakeholder engagement events. The Central Bank also seeks views of stakeholders including from consumer representatives and members of the public on the key risk drivers for consumers identified in the Central Bank's Outlook reports. Views and insights are used to inform the development of the following year's risk assessment and Outlook report. The Central Bank also conducts ad-hoc engagement with consumer representatives, for example when developing outreach activities.

The Central Bank regularly engages with consumer representatives and members of the public during public consultations on proposed changes to the legislative framework. On selected consultations, the Central Bank uses a third-party online tool and develops a simplified questionnaire directed to members of the public. Recently this online tool has been used on the Review of the Mortgage Measures Framework (Central Bank of Ireland, 2022[42]) and during engagement on the Discussion Paper on the Review of the Code (Central Bank of Ireland, 2022[5]). The Central Bank received 4 107 and 1 228 responses, respectively. The Central Bank has also used paid promotions on social media to publicise key consultations and raise awareness with members of the public.

While the Central Bank does not have a role in receiving, mediating or adjudicating on individual consumer complaints, the Central Bank reflects information received from consumers in its supervisory work. For example:

- the Central Bank launched the Tracker Mortgage Examination (described in Box 2.4) in 2015 after it became clear, through combined supervisory and enforcement work and from information supplied by consumer advocates, members of the public and public representatives, that tracker related issues could potentially be industrywide.
- the Central Bank engaged with a number of representative bodies and business owners in order to understand the importance of business interruption insurance in the context of Covid-19 and the impact of insurance firms' approaches on policy holders.

Engagement with small and medium sized enterprises

The Central Bank engages with small and medium-sized enterprises (SMEs) where material risks arise in relation to this cohort of consumers. For example, in the context of the consolidation in the retail banking market (see Box 2.3) the Central Bank proactively engaged directly with the Small Firms Association and the Irish Farmers Association on issues that directly impacted that sector, including their experiences on account migration, business lending and direct debits.

More broadly, the Small Firms Association is invited to attend any significant engagement event relevant to its members and the Central Bank also accepts invitations from the Small Firms Association and similar bodies to participate in their own engagement events. Additionally, in its regional outreach events, the Central Bank routinely meets with local Chambers of Commerce and small business representatives to exchange views and hear about relevant developments across the country to further inform its work. This structured approach allows the Central Bank to meet with a range of companies and not just those providing financial services.

Engagement with industry representatives and/or professional bodies

The Financial Industry Forum is a cross-sectoral, strategic forum for dialogue between the financial sector and the Central Bank. It is chaired by the Governor of the Central Bank, comprises 14 representative bodies across financial services; and meets twice per year. Three subgroups focus on domestic issues, international issues and innovation (including in each case consumer protection) and also meet twice per year.

As part of the engagement plan on consumer protection issues, the Central Bank regularly seeks views from the industry at a sectoral level including through regular bilateral engagements with industry bodies. The Central Bank also organises events with industry body members. For example, the Retail Intermediaries Roadshow (Central Bank of Ireland, 2023[43]) is a way to communicate key messages to the retail intermediary sector, identify issues and respond to questions. The roadshow is held in two locations across Ireland and around 450-500 people participate each year, including authorised retail intermediaries and representatives from industry bodies.

Finally, the Central Bank engages with small businesses and their representatives through regional visits, roundtables and other engagements on issues relevant to them, including consumer protection.

Engagement with other national oversight bodies

The Central Bank engages regularly with other national oversight bodies, and there are information sharing and co-operation arrangements in place.

- The Central Bank and the Financial Services and Pensions Ombudsman (FSPO) entered into a new Memorandum of Understanding (MoU) at the end of 2023, replacing the existing one, to increase mutual co-operation and information sharing. The MoU is an official framework that formalises reciprocal information exchange so that both parties co-operate and communicate constructively. This supports both parties in carrying out their respective but complementary functions effectively through regular engagements and information sharing, both formal and informal. It includes (amongst others) a process for the Central Bank to receive referrals from the FSPO (see more information on this in section 2.12).
- In 2021 the Central Bank and the Competition and Consumer Protection Commission (CCPC) renewed their existing co-operation agreement establishing a framework for co-operation, including regular meetings, and arrangements to share information (such as trends or serious cases of firms' behaviour harming consumers, market intelligence and research). In practice, the Central Bank and the CCPC engage frequently at senior and operational levels across a range of issues, for example in relation to account migration following the departure of two of the five main retail banks from the Irish market, financial education initiatives, and merger and acquisitions that impact the competitiveness of the Irish financial system.

Engagement with EU and international counterparts and international organisations

The Central Bank regularly engages with international counterparts. The Central Bank has entered into over 100 bilateral and multilateral MoUs with other national competent authorities and international bodies. Moreover, the Central Bank participates in several international fora that address financial consumer protection, including the International Financial Consumer Protection Organisation (FinCoNet).

The Central Bank is also part of the European System of Financial Supervision, which aims to ensure consistent and coherent financial supervision in the EU. The Central Bank participates in various groups and committees of the three European Supervisory Authorities (EBA, ESMA and EIOPA) and sits on the Board of Supervisors (the main decision-making body) of each.

Open and Engaged Charter

In July 2024, the Central Bank published an "Open and Engaged" Charter setting out its approach to stakeholder engagement (Central Bank of Ireland, 2024[44]). The Charter acknowledges that in a changing world, it is essential that the Central Bank is engaged with those who affect and are affected by its work, transparent in its decisions and policy-making, and open to new insights and diverse perspectives.

2.2.12. Facilitating innovation

The Central Bank has several mechanisms to facilitate innovation. In 2018 the Central Bank established the Innovation Hub to provide a platform to engage informally with innovators and for the Central Bank to learn about innovation. Since 2018, the Innovation Hub met with 375 innovators, fintech companies, innovation facilitators, regulated entities, and thought leaders (Central Bank of Ireland, 2022[45]). A diverse range of firms engage with the Innovation Hub, ranging from very small early-stage start-ups to large global firms. Although innovative firms of all sizes can engage with the Innovation Hub, most interactions are with start-up companies seeking to discuss regulations, to help them determine if, and where, they might fit in the regulatory landscape. The Innovation Hub is complemented by fintech and innovation events and an outreach programme where the Central Bank brings together individuals and companies involved in fintech and innovation with Central Bank staff.

In 2021 the Central Bank launched a review of its Innovation Hub. The review consisted of desk research on related initiatives of peer authorities and was informed by discussion in the innovation subgroup of the Financial Industry Forum, and broad engagement with stakeholders. As a result of this review, the Central Bank published a Consultation Paper seeking views on its approach to innovation engagement in financial services which closed in February 2024. This consultation set out proposals to evolve the approach through which the Central Bank engages with the innovation ecosystem and to promote better outcomes for society and the financial system, by:

- enhancing the Central Bank Innovation Hub to deliver deeper, clearer and more informed engagement with the innovation ecosystem.
- establishing an Innovation Sandbox Programme, which will involve informing the early-stage development of selected innovative initiatives (which are consistent with public policy objectives) by providing regulatory advice and support by within the programme.

Enhancements of the Central Bank Innovation Hub have already begun with the launch of the updated structured engagement process with the Innovation Hub and a refreshed Innovation Hub website page also now live. In July 2024, the Central Bank announced the theme of the first Innovation Sandbox Programme as “Combatting Financial Crime”. The Sandbox will commence in December 2024 and focus on the use of innovative technology to foster and develop solutions that minimise fraud, enhance KYC/AML/CFT frameworks, and improve day-to-day transaction security for consumers.

2.2.13. Professional standards

The Central Bank has standards relating to the professionalism of its staff. These include the Central Bank's Code of Ethics defining the standards, key principles and obligations for its employees, which include: i) act with integrity and prudence, ii) treat others with dignity and respect, iii) manage conflicts of interest, iv) protect confidentiality, v) represent the Central Bank appropriately and vi) report wrongdoing (Central Bank of Ireland, 2023[46]). The Central Bank has also developed a policy on managing conflicts of interest, a policy on staff trading of financial assets and a policy on receipt of business hospitality and gifts.

2.3. Principle 3: Access and inclusion

Principle 3 supports consumers' access and use of financial products and services to promote an inclusive financial system. This involves addressing barriers preventing consumers from accessing formal, regulated financial services while also protecting consumers during financial hardship or other circumstances leading to financial exclusion. Policy makers and oversight bodies are encouraged to incorporate financial inclusion and consumer protection objectives into strategies and policies relating to innovation, recognising that consumers may have varying digital skills and preferences and thus protecting access to cash and traditional financial services for some individuals.

2.3.1. Role of the Central Bank relating to Principle 3

While the Central Bank does not have an explicit statutory role in respect of ensuring consumers' access to financial services, financial inclusion can be supported with regulation that encourages firms to place the best interests of consumers at the heart of their commercial decision making, which is within the Central Bank's remit. Some sectoral regulations also impose requirements on regulated entities relating to access and inclusion where the Central Bank is the competent authority for the supervision and enforcement of compliance with those regulations.

In addition to supervision and enforcement of relevant regulations, the Central Bank can also advocate for measures to address consumers' challenges relating to access and inclusion. The Central Bank can also develop codes of conduct and regulations setting out requirements and expectations on regulated entities that they do not prevent access to basic financial services. For example, Box 2.2 provides a description of recent work done by the Central Bank to support consumers in a changing economic environment.

Box 2.2. Supporting consumers in a changing economic environment

Inflation in Ireland rose significantly from 2.4% in 2021 (Central Bank of Ireland, 2022[47]) to 8.1% in 2022 (Central Bank of Ireland, 2023[48]). At the same time, in response to building underlying inflationary pressures, the European Central Bank increased interest rates. The Central Bank of Ireland identified that the changing economic environment would pose challenges to consumers and undertook a number of actions from a consumer protection perspective.

In November 2022, the Central Bank issued a "Dear CEO" letter (Central Bank of Ireland, 2022[49]) to all regulated firms to reaffirm its expectations on how they should treat consumers in a changing economic landscape. The letter did not set out new regulatory requirements, but highlighted aspects of the regulatory framework that the Central Bank wished firms across various sectors to pay particular attention to, including the importance of:

- firms being able to identify consumers in vulnerable circumstances, including financial difficulty, and provide them with appropriate supports
- explaining the impact of inflation on investments
- operational resilience of payment mechanisms
- providing understandable information on the implications of any reduction or cancellation in insurance cover driven by affordability concerns.

The Central Bank also produced a consumer-targeted campaign on short-term credit in November 2022 (Central Bank of Ireland, 2022[50]). The purpose was to inform consumers of regulated firms' obligations, and build awareness of the implications of buying goods on short-term credit. The campaign was timed to coincide with the Black Friday/Cyber Monday online promotional period, ahead of the Christmas shopping period.

In April 2023, the Central Bank published research indicating that the impact of interest rate changes varied widely across Irish households. At the same time, the Central Bank published a note (Central Bank of Ireland, 2023[30]) setting out its ongoing work in relation to mortgages given the economic environment to ensure that:

- firms are operationally ready to identify and support borrowers who may face challenges meeting their repayments

- firms have sufficient operational capacity in place to manage applications by borrowers to switch their mortgage or mortgage provider and, where borrowers look to switch, there is no discrimination based on where they have their current loan (including in the case of borrowers with non-lending firms)
- interest rate increases are in line with loan terms and conditions, published variable rate policy statements and the regulatory framework for which the Central Bank is responsible.

To continue the Central Bank's focus on protecting consumers in a changing economic landscape, in early 2024 the Central Bank completed a Thematic Review on Early Mortgage Arrears, focussing on how firms are engaging with borrowers in or facing early arrears. The review assessed the effectiveness of the borrower journey, with a particular focus on engagement and communications in line with the consumer protection framework of the CCMA and Code (Central Bank of Ireland, 2024[51]). In April 2024 the Central Bank issued a "Dear CEO letter" (Central Bank of Ireland, 2024[51]) and published education content on its website targeting consumers to highlight how the consumer protection framework supports borrowers in or facing arrears (Central Bank of Ireland, 2024[52]).

2.3.2. Standards and requirements

Ireland has a number of regulatory requirements relating to access and inclusion. The European Union (Payment Accounts) Regulations 2016 set out the rules relating to the transparency and comparability of fees charged to consumers on their payment accounts, the right to access a payment account with basic features, the switching of payment accounts and the opening of cross-border payment accounts.

The Code provides that firms must ensure that, in all dealings with customers and within the context of their authorisation, they do not prevent access to basic financial services (without prejudice to the pursuit of legitimate commercial aims) through policies, procedures, or working practices. The Code also imposes obligations on regulated firms to ensure that vulnerable customers are provided with reasonable arrangements and assistance to facilitate dealings with firms. For example, the Code sets out requirements for banks when planning to close, merge or move a branch. These include the requirement to notify the Central Bank of any plans, to give at least two months' notice to affected consumers, and to notify the wider community. Moreover, as part of the ongoing review of the Code, the Central Bank has sought feedback on two areas relating to access and inclusion, namely "Availability and Choice" and "Firms Acting in Consumers' Best Interest".

The CCMA sets out the requirements for regulated entities on the treatment of consumers experiencing or expecting to experience difficulties in repaying their mortgage loans on primary residence, and the Code sets out requirements for firms on the handling of arrears in relation to non-mortgage lending and mortgage loans on non-primary residences.

2.3.3. Supervisory activity of the Central Bank

The Central Bank undertakes activity to ensure that regulated firms' commercial decisions take into account the impact on access to basic financial services. While decisions relating to the business model of regulated firms are commercial matters for the boards of firms, the Central Bank expects firms to take a consumer-focused approach concerning any decision that affects their customers. An examples of these activities includes the Central Bank's work in relation to branch closures. When banks decide to close branches, the Central Bank ensures that they comply with the requirements in the Code (as described above). The Central Bank requires banks to carry out and share with the Central Bank a Customer Impact Assessment (CIA) assessing risks to consumers arising from the closure of the branch and setting out mitigating measures. The CIA may include an analysis of customers' behaviours and their engagement across distribution channels, an analysis of alternative options available to consumers, considerations for vulnerable customers and a stakeholder engagement plan. Where gaps in the mitigation strategy are identified, the Central Bank can require banks to put additional measures in place to mitigate risks to consumers. The Central Bank also communicated to retail banks its expectations when they plan to close, merge and move branches, including conducting ex-post assessments 9 to 15 months after the change and rectifying any material issues.

Regarding access to cash and branch closures, the Central Bank also responded to the public consultation launched by the Department of Finance as a result of the Retail Banking Review (Department of Finance, 2022[53]). In its response, the Central Bank discussed recent trends and structural developments relating to access to cash in Ireland and argued for the need to discuss social policy objectives of issues arising (Central Bank of Ireland, 2022[18]). In July 2024 the Department of Finance published the Finance (Provision of Access to Cash Infrastructure) Bill 2024 which aims to ensure that sufficient and effective access to cash is available in Ireland, and that any further evolution of the cash infrastructure will be managed in a fair, orderly, transparent and equitable manner for all stakeholders (Department of Finance, 2024[54]).]

In 2022 the Central Bank continued its work to ensure that consumers are given appropriate support when switching providers. This included ongoing supervisory engagement with the five main retail banks to ensure that they had plans in place to manage the impact on consumers of the departure of Ulster Bank and KBC Bank, two of Ireland's five main retail banks at that time, which were exiting the retail banking sector (see Box 2.3). As a co-ordinated approach across the sector was essential to ensure good customer experience and continuity of services, in 2022 the Central Bank arranged a series of meetings with the CEOs of the five main retail banks and the Banking & Payments Federation Ireland (BPFI), an industry association. The Central Bank also discussed arrangements with the largest direct debit originators that are regulated by the Central Bank (e.g. insurance companies) to ensure continuity of service in case of issues relating to the payments of direct debits. The Central Bank regularly published statistics to monitor the migration. The final statistics on account migration were published in July 2023. At the end of June 2023, 96% of the 1.2m accounts that were open with Ulster Bank and KBC Bank at the beginning of 2022 were either closed or inactive (Central Bank of Ireland, 2023[55]).

Box 2.3. Consolidation in Ireland's retail banking market

In early 2021 two large retail banks, Ulster Bank, a subsidiary of NatWest Group, and KBC Bank Ireland, a subsidiary of KBC Group, announced their plans to exit the Irish market. This resulted in the closure of more than 1.2m accounts requiring customers to migrate to another bank.

In June 2021 and April 2022 the Central Bank published two "Dear CEO" letters addressed to both the remaining and the departing banks setting out its expectations on the treatment of consumers at a time of change in the retail banking landscape (Central Bank of Ireland, 2021[56]; 2022[57]). These included the need for transparency and effective disclosure including as regards notice periods, the need for specific and effective processes and communication plans to support vulnerable customers and ongoing responsibility for errors and complaints handling. In anticipation of an increase in customer engagement levels during this period, the Central Bank also commenced a review of the retail banks' performance on customer support phone lines in 2021. Based on the review, the Central Bank required the retail banks to put new measures and resources in place to improve customer service.

Finally, another example of the activity of the Central Bank relating to access and inclusion is its work since 2020 concerning mortgage arrears (Central Bank of Ireland, 2022[58]). Going back to the 2008 financial crisis, the Central Bank put a consumer protection framework in place dedicated to dealing with accounts in or facing mortgage arrears, with the CCMA providing the framework for mortgage arrears on primary residences. However, despite a gradual decrease, the level of mortgage accounts in long-term (i.e. over a year) mortgage arrears (LTMA) remained elevated (around 30,000 principal dwelling house (PDH) mortgage accounts in LTMA at the end of 2020). Moreover, research conducted over a sample of borrowers in LTMA highlights significant levels of financial distress, as these individuals had an average ratio of debt service burdens to net income around 61% (with a median of 43%), higher levels of negative equity compared to the wider population and their levels of spending were below the recommended levels for reasonable living standards (Kelly et al., 2021[59]).

Since 2020, the Central Bank has undertaken extensive supervisory engagement and data analysis to improve the resolution of LTMA focussing on non-lending credit firms (NLFs) that hold the largest proportion of LTMA accounts. The Central Bank scrutinised the activities of firms in relation to different borrower categories based on repayments patterns. Special focus was placed on firms' steps to resolve LTMA for borrowers classified by the firm as co-operating and paying towards their mortgage, while also requiring firms to continue to work on engagement strategies with remaining borrowers. The Central Bank required firms to submit data on a regular basis including the financial hardship arrangements employed. As of December 2023, there were around 20 000 PDH mortgage accounts in LTMA. The Central Bank continues to monitor NLFs' progress in this area and hold them to account on their progress.

The Central Bank also highlighted in the Consumer Protection Outlook Report published in 2023 its concerns and expectations for firms where consumers lack digital literacy or access to digital tools which may create barriers for consumers (Central Bank of Ireland, 2023[60]).

2.4. Principle 4: Financial Literacy and Awareness

Principle 4 promotes financial literacy and awareness as part of a broader strategy for financial inclusion. It suggests that stakeholders should develop mechanisms to help consumers acquire the knowledge, skills and attitudes necessary to understand financial risks and opportunities, make informed decisions, seek assistance when needed and take effective actions to support their financial well-being. These mechanisms may include enhancing digital financial literacy skills and raising awareness of digital security risks. Financial literacy programmes should be easily accessible through various channels, including digital platforms, and should cater to all age groups. Additionally, it is encouraged to conduct national and international data collection exercises and stakeholders should implement the principles, guidelines and methodologies on financial literacy developed by the OECD International Network on Financial Education (INFE).

2.4.1. Role of the Central Bank and other public stakeholders relating to Principle 4

As a result of the recommendations included in the Retail Banking Review (Department of Finance, 2022[53]), the Department of Finance is developing a national strategy for financial literacy (National Strategy) in co-ordination with key stakeholders (see below). The Department of Finance launched a public consultation in August 2023 (Department of Finance, 2023[61]), published a Mapping Report in April 2024 and plans to publish the National Strategy in early 2025 (Department of Finance, 2024[62]).

The key stakeholder in financial education is the Competition and Consumer Protection Commission (CCPC). The CCPC has a statutory responsibility to provide information about personal finance products to consumers and to promote financial education and capability. The CCPC adopts the principles, guidelines and methodologies developed by the INFE and regularly conducts or commissions research to inform public awareness campaigns and design financial education programmes. Examples include the annual CCPC Pension Research (Competition and Consumer Protection Commission, 2022[63]), the behavioural research on savings products conducted in collaboration with the Behavioural Research Unit of the Economic and Social Research Institute (ESRI) (Timmons, Robertson and Lunn, 2022[64]), the research into influencer marketing (Competition and Consumer Protection Commission, 2023[65]), and the report on financial wellbeing in Ireland (Competition and Consumer Protection Commission, 2023[66])

The Central Bank does not have a statutory function relating to financial literacy and awareness. However, the Central Bank regularly conducts consumer awareness and educational initiatives in line with its mandate to ensure the proper and effective regulation of financial services providers and markets, while ensuring that the best interests of consumers of financial services are protected. Among these, the Central Bank established the Consumer Hub as a dedicated section of its website which serves as a resource for consumers to access information and support on financial matters with the objective of offering clear and impartial information to consumers to help them make informed decisions. The Consumer Hub provides guidance on various topics including banking, insurance, mortgages and investment via different means, such as videos, text and frequently asked questions (Central Bank of Ireland, 2024[67]). This content is promoted across digital channels and through paid digital media to reach a broad consumer audience.

The Central Bank also publishes warnings about developments in financial services, including scams and frauds, such as warnings relating to the purchase of crypto-assets (Central Bank of Ireland, 2022[68]) and warnings about an "advance fee fraud" scam targeting consumers applying for loans by offering a loan in exchange for an upfront or administration fee (Central Bank of Ireland, 2023[69]). The Central Bank also publishes educational resources targeted to younger people and conducts public awareness campaigns such as the campaign across national broadcast and digital channels called "How can I protect myself from financial scams?" to inform the public on how to recognise a potential scam. The Central Bank also developed a SAFE test (Stop, Assess, Fact-check, and Expose and report) designed to help consumers to protect themselves from scams (Central Bank of Ireland, 2023[70]).

Other campaigns launched by the Central Bank include campaigns to inform consumers about saving money, mortgage arrears and financial difficulty (Central Bank of Ireland, 2022[71]), and the risks of buying goods and services using short-term credit. The short term credit campaign was launched in November 2022, at the same time as the introduction of new legislation requiring the authorisation of providers of hire-purchase, personal contract plans, consumer hire and credit-like agreements (such as Buy Now Pay Later or BNPL services) (Central Bank of Ireland, 2022[50]). In November 2023, the Central Bank also launched a campaign targeting consumers considering using BNPL to make purchases ahead of the Christmas shopping period (Central Bank of Ireland, 2023[72]).

2.4.2. Co-ordination arrangements

The Central Bank co-ordinates with the CCPC on matters related to financial literacy and awareness as part of the co-operation agreement existing between the two authorities (see section 2.2.11 for more details on the co-operation agreement between the Central Bank and the CCPC).

2.5. Principle 5: Competition

Principle 5 promotes fair, efficient, and competitive retail financial markets and stipulates that consumers should have the ability to easily search for, compare and switch between products and providers. For competition to work well, consumers need to be able to access, assess and act on the information about the products and services they purchase. When consumers can make informed decisions, they are able to select the products offering the best value for them. In turn, active and informed consumers create the incentives for firms to offer better value products.

2.5.1. Role of the Central Bank and other public stakeholders relating to Principle 5

The Central Bank does not have a role in promoting competition in financial services markets. However, when performing and exercising its powers, the Central Bank is required to do so in a way that is consistent with the orderly and proper functioning of financial markets as explained in its Annual Report and Annual Performance Statement. In addition, the Central Bank is the competent authority to supervise and ultimately enforce certain provisions relating to competition, namely supporting consumers when switching financial products and services. The following paragraphs provide details on such provisions. The CCPC is responsible for enforcing competition law in Ireland. The CCPC has powers to investigate and impose sanctions for infringements of competition law, to administer Ireland's merger control regime and to advocate for consideration of competition issues in public policy. The co-operation agreement between the Central Bank and the CCPC provides a framework within which the two authorities may exchange information, including in relation to the CCPC's competition functions.

2.5.2. Standards and requirements

Ireland's financial consumer protection framework includes several mechanisms relating to switching between financial products and services. Some of these are supervised and enforced by the CCPC, others by the Central Bank. Mechanisms to facilitate consumers' ability to search and compare between financial products and services fall under the responsibility of the CCPC. Moreover, the European Union (Payment Accounts) Regulations 2016 requires the CCPC to operate a price comparison website allowing consumers to compare fees charged by payment services providers for at least a selected list of services charged by payment services providers.

The Central Bank is the competent authority to supervise and enforce the provisions included in the European Union (Payment Accounts) Regulations 2016 relating to switching of payment accounts and opening of cross-border payment accounts. The Central Bank has set out further obligations in the Code of Conduct on the Switching of Payment Accounts with Payment Service Providers.

In June 2018, the Central Bank made specific changes to the Code to introduce provisions that would make it easier for consumers to switch between financial service providers by ensuring that consumers were provided with certain information in relation to their outstanding mortgage (Central Bank of Ireland, 2018[73]). These changes to the Code place obligations on firms to make mortgage switching easier for consumers, for example by requiring firms to tell consumers about cheaper mortgage options 60 days before coming out of a fixed rate period or on an annual basis for variable rate mortgage holders, to explain benefits and risks of any mortgage incentives such as cashback offers, to give consumers (at their request) a comparison of the monetary costs of their mortgage compared to other options and to give consumers a decision on their application within ten business days of receiving a completed mortgage application.

In recent years, the Central Bank has undertaken consumer research to understand how to make it easier for customers to compare mortgages and identify potential cost savings (Byrne, Devine and Mccarthy, 2022[74]). Building on this, the Central Bank is currently proposing new requirements on the provision of information to enhance internal switching (i.e. switching to another mortgage product of the current provider) in the ongoing review of the Code. Lenders will have to include within the annual mortgage notifications a personalised euro savings estimate alongside each alternative mortgage refinancing option presented. Additionally, lenders will be required to provide a specific reminder to customers concerning mortgage refinancing options, issued between four and eight weeks from the first notification.

Other initiatives to promote a better switching environment include proposals to require insurance companies to give two pre-renewal notifications to customers, and that certain types of insurance (i.e. gadget insurance, travel insurance, dental insurance, and pet insurance) can only be renewed automatically when customers have expressly agreed to.

The Central Bank is also engaging with mortgage providers via the Banking & Payments Federation Ireland (BPFI) to examine how certain barriers to mortgage switching can be overcome (Central Bank of Ireland, 2024[6]). This would involve identifying any common process enhancements amongst lenders that could be reflected in an industry protocol or charter. Examples of the activity of the Central Bank relating to competition include the work to protect consumers in a changing economic environment (see Box 2.2). As part of this work, the Central Bank required firms to have sufficient operational capacity in place to manage applications by borrowers to switch their mortgage or mortgage provider and, when borrowers look to switch, firms must ensure there is no discrimination based on where they have their current loan.

2.6. Principle 6: Equitable and Fair Treatment of Consumers

Principle 6 stipulates the importance of treating all consumers fairly, honestly and equitably throughout their interactions with financial services providers and intermediaries. Fair treatment should be ingrained in the governance and culture of firms, with the increasing use of digital technology ensuring that such advancements do not result in discriminatory outcomes for consumers. Particular attention should be given to consumers experiencing vulnerability, which can arise from various personal, economic and market circumstances. Approaches to address vulnerability vary and could involve providing impartial debt advice to those facing financial hardship due to excessive debt burdens.

2.6.1. Role of the Central Bank and other public stakeholders relating to Principle 6

The Central Bank is the competent authority for the supervision and enforcement of regulations related to the equitable and fair treatment of consumers. Other stakeholders playing an important role relating to Principle 6 include:

- the Money Advice and Budgeting Service (MABS). MABS is a free, confidential service that provides advice and support to individuals experiencing financial difficulties. MABS offers personalised guidance on managing money, budgeting effectively, dealing with debts, and accessing financial assistance programmes. The service is available to anyone in Ireland facing financial challenges, regardless of their income level or background. Additionally, MABS conducts outreach programmes and educational initiatives to promote financial literacy and awareness within communities.
- the Free Legal Advice Centres (FLAC). FLAC is an independent not-for-profit non-governmental organisation dedicated to the realisation of equal justice for all. FLAC provides free legal information to members and conducts legal analysis and law reform campaigning, across a range of areas including debt, credit and financial services.
- the Insolvency Service of Ireland (ISI). The ISI is a government agency established to help individuals and businesses in Ireland manage unsustainable debt situations. Its primary goal is to restore insolvent persons to solvency, supporting people struggling with debt and facilitating fair and orderly arrangements between debtors and creditors. The ISI oversees several debt relief mechanisms, including i) the Personal Insolvency Arrangement (PIA), which is a formal agreement between a debtor and their creditors to restructure or settle debts, typically lasting 6-7 years; ii) the Debt Settlement Arrangement (DSA), which is similar to a PIA but for unsecured debts, allowing for a negotiated settlement over 5 years; and iii) the Debt Relief Notice (DRN), which provides relief from qualifying unsecured debts for individuals with low income and assets, subject to certain criteria.

Moreover, the Equal Status Acts 2010-2018 prohibit discrimination on certain grounds (gender, marital status, family status, age, disability, sexual orientation, race, religion and membership in the traveller community). Concerning disability, discrimination can include a refusal or failure by the firm to do all that is reasonable to accommodate the needs of a person with a disability by providing special treatment or facilities, if without such special treatment or facilities, it would be impossible or unduly difficult for the consumer to access the service or product. The Acts apply across the provision of goods and services in Ireland, including the provision of financial services. The Irish Human Rights and Equality Commission (IHREC) is an independent body set up under the Equal Status Acts to promote and protect human rights and equality in Ireland.

2.6.2. Standards and requirements

Financial regulation imposes obligations on financial services providers regarding equitable and fair treatment of consumers and the Central Bank is the competent authority for the supervision and enforcement of compliance with these requirements. They include, for example, provisions in the IDR and in MiFID II Regulations requiring insurance distributors and MiFID investment firms to act honestly, fairly and professionally in the best interest of their customers.

In addition, as described in section 2.1.2, the General Principles of the Code state that regulated firms must i) act in the best interest of customers and in the integrity of the market, ii) act honestly, fairly and professionally, and iii) act with due skills, care and diligence. The Code also requires firms to provide vulnerable consumers with reasonable and necessary arrangements and/or assistance to facilitate consumers' dealings with firms.

The Code requires regulated firms to ensure that advertising is clear, fair, accurate and not misleading. Moreover, Central Bank Codes may also impose specific obligations relevant to firms in particular sectors. For example:

- in the context of insurance, the Code includes provisions requiring firms to offer fair settlement to claimants, taking into account all relevant factors and representing the firm's best estimate of the claimant's reasonable entitlement.
- as set out in section 2.1.2, the CCMA imposes obligations on firms when dealing with borrowers in arrears, or who are likely to go into arrears.

2.6.3. Guidance

As part of the review of the Code, the Central Bank is preparing guidance for firms in relation to how to approach the obligation to act in the best interests of customers by securing their customers' interests, and guidance on how to secure the interests of consumers in vulnerable circumstances. The latter guidance includes a definition of vulnerability and sets out an approach for firms in approaching the issue of vulnerability and providing assistance to consumers in vulnerable circumstances. In addition, the Central Bank's Guide on Consumer Protection Risk Assessment sets out guidance as regards firms' risk management frameworks, including firm monitoring to ensure that fair outcomes are being achieved. Finally, the Central Bank's Regulatory and Supervisory Outlook sets expectations that regulated firms should act to identify, mitigate and manage drivers of risks to consumers. For example, where errors or operational incidents have occurred, the Central Bank expects regulated firms to treat consumers fairly and restore them to the position they would have been in had the error or incident not occurred.

2.6.4. Supervisory activity of the Central Bank

The supervisory frameworks described in section 2.2.4 provide the structure for the Central Bank's supervisory approach with respect to equitable and fair treatment of consumers. Risks to the equitable and fair treatment of consumers in particular sectors are identified through the sectoral risk assessment process and the approach to addressing these risks is set out in multi-year strategies for each sector.

An example of the supervisory activity of the Central Bank relating to equitable and fair treatment of consumers is the work on price walking in home and motor insurance markets. Having identified the risk that insurers might be unfairly taking advantage of consumers' behaviours and habits, in 2021, the Central Bank undertook a review to understand how differential pricing was used in the private car and home insurance markets in Ireland. This included an extensive analysis of documents submitted by firms, a large consumer insights survey, and statistical analysis of policy records across a three-year period. Based on this review the Central Bank concluded that certain practices could result in unfair outcomes for some consumers. The Central Bank therefore banned price walking in these markets on the basis that such pricing practices lacked transparency and exploited consumer inertia and ultimately undermine consumer trust and harm their financial well-being (Central Bank of Ireland, 2021[33]). In December 2023 the Central Bank published a report on the impact of the ban, which found that consumers who remain with their current provider are no longer paying a loyalty penalty (Central Bank of Ireland, 2023[75]).

2.7. Principle 7: Disclosure and Transparency

Principle 7 stipulates that financial services firms should provide consumers with essential information regarding the benefits, risks and terms of financial products and services, irrespective of the distribution channel. Disclosure of information should cover material aspects of the product or service as well as the potential conflicts of interest associated with the intermediaries selling the product or service. Information disclosed should be accurate, honest, transparent and non-misleading. Standardised pre-contractual disclosure should be adopted to facilitate comparison between products and tailored disclosure mechanism should appropriately take into account product complexity and risks. Consumer research and behavioural insights should inform the design of disclosure requirements and help consumers to make informed decisions.

2.7.1. Standards and requirements

The Central Bank is responsible for the supervision and enforcement of provisions imposing requirements on firms relating to disclosure and transparency. Such requirements are included in sectoral and cross-section legislation and in various codes of conducts.

Disclosure and transparency requirements for financial services and products are set out in sectoral legislation including the European Union (Insurance Distribution) Regulations 2018, the Consumer Insurance Contracts Act 2019, the Non-Life Insurance (Provision of Information) Regulations 2007, the Life Assurance (Provision of Information) Regulations 2001 for insurance products, the European Union (Payment Services) Regulations 2018 (PSR) for payment services, the European Union (Markets in Financial Instruments) Regulations 2017 and Regulation (EU) on Key Information Documents for Packaged Retail and Insurance-Based Investment Products for retail investment products, the European Union (Consumer Mortgage Credit Agreements) Regulations 2016 and the European Communities (Consumer Credit Agreements) Regulations 2010. The last two introduce mandatory provision of standardised pre-contractual information to consumers using the European Standardised Information Sheet (ESIS) and the Standard European Consumer Credit Information form (SECCI), respectively.

Disclosure requirements concerning prospectuses for UCITS and RIAIFs (investment funds that may be marketed to retail investors) are set out in the European Communities (Undertakings for Collective Investment in Transferable Securities) Regulations 2011; Central Bank (Supervision and Enforcement) Act 2013 (Section 48(1)) (Undertakings for Collective Investment in Transferable Securities) Regulations 2019; and the AIF Rulebook. Fund disclosure is reviewed by the Central Bank prior to authorisation as described in section 2.1.4.

Regarding the codes of conduct, the Code requires regulated firms to provide information to consumers on a durable medium "*about the main features and restrictions of the product to assist the consumer in understanding the product*". Regulated firms are also required to provide consumers with the terms and conditions of the product before they enter into a contract for that product. In addition, the Code also sets out the information that an insurance company or intermediary must provide when quoting a product including, but not limited to, the value of the quotation, the time validity, and any discounts applied. Regarding sectoral codes, the CCMA sets out requirements regarding the provision of information to borrowers in arrears.

In addition, the European Banking Authority (EBA), the European Securities and Market Authority (ESMA), and the European Insurance and Occupational Pensions Authority (EIOPA) have issued guidelines requiring regulated firms to conduct testing of their products before distribution to ensure that consumers can understand terms and conditions.

2.7.2. Guidance

The Central Bank provides guidance to firms relating to disclosure and transparency in several ways, including in the Outlook publications that set out expectations to firms and examples of good practices and "Dear CEO" letters. In addition, the Central Bank's Guide to Consumer Protection Risk Assessment sets out examples of good practices for firms on explaining key product features and ensuring that consumers understand key product information as part of an effective consumer risk management framework.

2.7.3. Consumer testing and research

The Central Bank conducts consumer testing and research and collects data to understand consumers' decision-making and choices. The findings of the research are used for diagnostic work, to develop and test the efficacy of potential regulatory interventions or to support the Central Bank's supervisory activity. Examples of consumer research include the work on attitude and behaviours of consumers of Buy Now Pay Later (BNPL) products (Central Bank of Ireland, 2023[76]), which identified a lack of understanding amongst consumers that BNPL is a form of credit rather than a payment arrangement. Section 2.8.3 provides more information on this work.

The Central Bank also conducts consumer research on many other topics. These include research on pension decumulation products to explore consumers' attitudes and behaviours towards pension funding and their understanding of decumulation options (Central Bank of Ireland, 2024[77]), on motor and home insurances as part of the work on differential pricing (Central Bank of Ireland, 2021[33]), on key information documents for packaged retail and insurance-based investment products (PRIIPs) and on inaction in the mortgage market (Byrne, Devine and Mccarthy, 2022[74]), where the Central Bank tested different versions of reminders sent to mortgage holders to encourage them to refinance their loans.

Finally, the Central Bank also conducted consumer research as part of its work related to the withdrawal of Ulster Bank and KBC Bank Ireland from Ireland's retail banking market. The research discussed approaches that financial institutions can use to increase consumer engagement in retail banking (Beere et al., 2022[78]).

The consultation paper on the Review of the Code includes a proposal to introduce a new requirement for regulated firms to monitor and review communications to their customers to ensure they are effective, meaningful and well understood, and that they facilitate customers' decision-making (Central Bank of Ireland, 2024[6]).

2.7.4. Supervisory activity of the Central Bank

The supervisory frameworks described in section 2.2.4 provide the structure for the Central Bank's supervisory approach with respect to transparency and disclosure. Risks related to transparency and disclosure in particular sectors are identified through the sectoral risk assessment process and the approach to addressing these risks is set out in multi-year supervisory strategies for each sector. An example of the supervisory activity of the Central Bank with respect to transparency and disclosure is thematic work on under-insurance in home insurance markets (Central Bank of Ireland, 2022[79]). An increase in construction costs led to an increase in levels of under-insurance which grew from 6.5% in 2017 to 16.5% in 2022. The Central Bank found that the way in which insurance firms presented and provided key information to consumers varied across firms, and some firms did not adequately communicate with their customers on a timely basis to ensure that they understood the risks of not having sufficient home insurance. The Central Bank issued a "Dear CEO" letter outlining its expectations that firms should clearly communicate to their customers about the risks of under-insurance.

Another example is an enforcement case involving a retail intermediary that did not communicate in a clear manner to its customers regarding fee structures and also overcharged certain customers. The Central Bank found that the intermediary overcharged 62 customers over a period of five years, and provided unclear communication on applicable fees to 190 customers. As a result, the Central Bank issued an RMP requiring the intermediary to refund all 62 customers that were overcharged and to amend its communications to customers as regards fees to make them clearer. In addition, the Central Bank reprimanded and fined the retail intermediary EUR 41 385 for breaches of its obligations under the Code. The decision is published on the Central Bank's website to send a wider message to firms and individuals in order to improve compliance, behaviour and culture across the financial system.

2.8. Principle 8: Quality Financial Products

Principle 8 relates to the design and distribution of financial products that align with the interests and objectives of consumers and improve their financial well-being. Adequate oversight and governance by financial services providers and intermediaries should include the implementation of systems to design, approve, manage and monitor financial products throughout their life cycle, ensuring compliance with regulatory requirements and meeting consumer needs. To promote quality and value for money for consumers, providers and intermediaries need to define target markets, conduct research, use behavioural insights and conduct testing before launching products considering complexity and risks.

2.8.1. Standards and requirements

The Central Bank is the competent authority for the supervision and enforcement of compliance with regulations imposing obligations relating to product governance. These include i) the EBA Guidelines on product oversight and governance arrangements for retail banking products, which set out the standards relating to the design of retail banking products to ensure they meet the interests and objectives of the target consumers, ii) the Insurance Distribution Directive product oversight and governance requirements, imposing obligations on firms to consider the best interest of consumers during product design and throughout the lifecycle of the product, including distribution complemented by EIOPA's approach to the supervision of product oversight and governance, and iii) MiFID II Regulations and ESMA's guidelines on MiFID II product governance requirements imposing obligations for firms to ensure that investment products and their distribution are designed to meet the needs of a target market.

The three European Supervisory Authorities have issued guidelines in their respective spheres that put in place obligations on manufacturers of products to ensure that effective product testing is carried out before financial products are distributed to the intended markets.

2.8.2. Guidance

The Central Bank provides guidance to firms relating to the quality of financial products in several ways, including setting out expectations to firms and examples of good practices in its Outlook publications and "Dear CEO" letters, for example following supervisory work. Moreover, as described in section 2.1.3, the Central Bank sets out examples of good product development practices within an effective consumer risk management framework in its Guide to CPRA (Central Bank of Ireland, 2017[21])

2.8.3. Consumer testing and research

The Central Bank regularly uses behavioural insights to inform its financial consumer protection supervisory functions relating to the quality of financial products. Relevant work includes the consumer research conducted on consumer understanding of BNPL products and on drivers of consumer behaviour in the motor and home insurance markets. In addition to the findings described in section 2.7.3, the consumer research on BNPL products found that Irish consumers appear to have limited experience of these products (15% of adults reported using or having used BNPL products). BNPL consumers tend to be younger and more likely to be female. BNPL products are typically used when shopping both in store and online. The research also showed that BNPL products appear to be associated with impulsive shopping or unplanned spending, and that 38% of BNPL users agree that BNPL has made them "more likely to purchase things they don't need" and 43% agree that they "often spend significantly more money than planned when they use BNPL".

2.8.4. Supervisory activity of the Central Bank

The Central Bank conducts supervision and enforcement activities related to the quality of financial products. The supervisory frameworks described in section 2.2.4 provide the structure for the Central Bank's supervisory approach in this regard. Risks related to product governance in particular sectors are identified through the sectoral risk assessment process and the approach to addressing these risks is set out in multi-year strategies for each sector.

An example of the Central Bank's supervisory activity in this area is the review of structured retail products, which was launched as risks from these products were identified as a concern as part of the Central Bank's internal sectoral risk assessment process, informed by a number of complaints received. The Central Bank conducted a series of reviews of structured retail products offered and distributed by MiFID investment firms and found failures by firms to consider potential difficulties consumers may have understanding some of the features of these products, and to present past performance information in a fair manner. To address these poor practices, the Central Bank issued a "Dear CEO" letter setting out its expectations relating to identifying the target market and use of complex features and disclosure (Central Bank of Ireland, 2022[36]), which was supplemented with further supervisory guidance in 2023 to ensure that expectations of firms were fully clear (Central Bank of Ireland, 2023[80]). Relevant firms were required to review their governance arrangements against these expectations and address any deficiencies identified.

In order to raise awareness amongst consumers of the complexity of and risks associated with these products, the Central Bank published an Explainer on its Consumer Hub. The Central Bank also communicated the findings of its review to the CCPC and supported the CCPC in enhancing the information on structured retail products on the CCPC's website.

2.9. Principle 9: Responsible Business Conduct and Culture of Financial Services Providers and Intermediaries

Principle 9 outlines how financial services providers and intermediaries should ensure they act in the best interest of consumers. To do this, providers should be accountable for the actions of their intermediaries, promoting fair treatment and financial well-being. When providing products or services, providers should assess consumers' capabilities, situations and needs, recommend suitable options and contribute to their well-being. Providers and intermediaries should be properly qualified and trained, avoid conflicts of interest, and ensure appropriate management when they arise. Financial advice should be objective, based on the consumer's profile and consider the complexity and risks associated with the product, as well as the consumer's financial objectives, knowledge, capabilities, and experience. Finally, remuneration structures should be transparently disclosed to consumers and designed to encourage responsible conduct and fair treatment.

2.9.1. Standards and requirements

The Central Bank is the competent authority for the supervision and enforcement of compliance with requirements for firms relating to the design and sale of suitable financial products. Legislation includes provisions relating to the assessment of suitability of a product for a specific customer or target market, the management of conflicts of interest, ensuring that people in key functions in regulated firms are fit and proper and ensuring that employees of regulated firms have the necessary skills, knowledge and qualification to carry out their function. The next paragraphs describe such legislation.

Regulated firms are required to be responsible for the actions of their intermediaries when the intermediary acts as an agent and it has been appointed by the regulated firm. However, intermediaries in Ireland are typically authorised and supervised by the Central Bank and they do not act under the responsibility of another entity, unless they are "tied agents". Moreover, the Central Bank published guidance on outsourcing, setting out the Central Bank's expectations and good practices to manage outsourcing risk (Central Bank of Ireland, 2021[81]).

Relating to the effective management of conflicts of interest, the MiFID II Regulations and the IDR require MiFID investment firms and insurance distributors to have mechanisms in place to identify, prevent and mitigate conflicts of interest. The MiFID II Regulations and the IDR also contain provisions related to the remuneration structures and to the monitoring of how the behaviour of employees may be affected by incentives. Finally, the F&P Regime requires that individuals in key and customer-facing roles are competent, capable, honest, ethical and of integrity.

Moreover, the Code contains a number of provisions relating to responsible business conduct, including provisions requiring firms to manage of conflicts of interest, to ensure that the remuneration structure i) does not undermine compliance with the firm's duty to act honestly, fairly and professionally and ii) is not linked to targets in contradiction with consumers' best interest (e.g., targets related to volume or bonus payments linked to business retention).

Relating to the provision of financial advice, the Code defines an intermediary as independent when the activities provided by the intermediary are based on a fair analysis of the market and when the intermediary does not accept any fees or commissions or other remuneration, other than a fee paid by the consumer (or a minor non-monetary benefit from a third party). The Code also requires that financial advice is suitable to the customer, i.e., it takes into account facts and circumstances disclosed by the customer.

More broadly, as set out in section 2.1.1, an Individual Accountability Framework has recently been introduced which will set out expected standards of conduct for individuals working within firms, complemented by Standards for Business which will apply to the firms themselves. The introduction of the Individual Accountability Framework follows recommendations from the Central Bank in its 2018 report on

Behaviour and Culture of the Irish Retail Banks aimed at improving governance, enhancing the culture of accountability in firms and achieving better outcomes for consumers (Central Bank of Ireland, 2018[82]).

2.9.2. Guidance

The Central Bank provides guidance to firms relating to responsible business conduct and culture in several ways. The Central Bank's Guide to Consumer Protection Risk Assessment sets out that one of the five modules of an appropriate consumer protection risk management framework is "people and culture". Positive practices identified by the Guide include for example that the firm can demonstrate, with clear examples, how leadership actions and communications are encouraging a culture of consumer protection throughout the firm.

In addition, the Central Bank's Outlook publications and "Dear CEO" letters set out expectations to firms and examples of good practices. Moreover, the Central Bank has issued guidance on its F&P Regime, which was last updated in December 2023 (Central Bank of Ireland, 2023[83]).

2.9.3. Supervisory activity of the Central Bank

The supervisory frameworks described in section 2.2.4 provide the structure for the Central Bank's supervisory approach with respect to responsible business conduct and culture. An example of the activity of the Central Bank relating to responsible business conduct and culture is the thematic work on ongoing suitability of long-term life insurance products conducted in 2023. The Central Bank identified the risk that insurance products designed to be held by policyholders for the medium-to-long term may become less suitable or unsuitable over time. To conduct this thematic work, the Central Bank gathered qualitative and quantitative information from a large sample of insurance providers and intermediaries. The Central Bank identified evidence of good and poor practices and processes in its assessment of the ongoing suitability of long-term insurance products. To communicate the results of its review, the Central Bank issued a "Dear CEO" letter to the life insurance sector and to the insurance intermediary sector (Central Bank of Ireland, 2023[84]). Another example of the activity of the Central Bank is the Tracker Mortgage Examination (see Box 2.4 for details on this work).

More broadly, many of the risks identified by the Central Bank are linked to firm culture. For example, as a result of the work on under-insurance in the home insurance market described in section 2.7.4, the Central Bank issued a "Dear CEO" letter noting that firms had different levels of maturity of their Consumer Protection Risk Management Frameworks and that firms were not sufficiently proactive in identifying risks for consumers and related mitigation strategies, raising concerns of a lack of consumer-focussed culture in firms.

Moreover, the "Dear CEO" letter issued by the Central Bank as part of its work on account migration described in Box 2.3 called out the importance of a consumer-focused culture in seeking to ensure that potential consumer risks arising from the departure of two retail banks did not materialise.

Box 2.4. The Tracker Mortgage Examination

Mortgages with tracker interest rates grew in popularity in Ireland between 2003 and 2008. When interest rates started to rise in the period leading to and following the Global Financial Crisis, all lenders stopped offering tracker rates to new customers.

However, by ceasing to offer tracker mortgages, some lenders failed to meet obligations they had to some of their existing customers. Affected customers can be broken down in two main categories. Sixty per cent of affected consumers were denied the contractual right or reasonable expectation of a tracker rate, for example at the end of a fixed interest rate period, and 21% were charged an interest rate with an incorrect implied margin, for example one that was different from the margin specified in the loan offer. The remaining 19% were affected by other related issues (such as a delay in reverting to the tracker interest rate at the end of the fixed rate period or lack of communication about changes in interest rates).

What did the Central Bank do?

Between 2008 and 2022, the Central Bank intervened by:

- requiring certain lenders to offer customers who had been affected the right to return to a tracker rate and/or payment of redress and compensation.
- strengthening the protections for customers with a tracker mortgage.
- launching the Tracker Mortgage Examination in 2015 (the final report was published in 2019). As part of the Examination, the Central Bank set out a framework requiring 15 lenders to systematically assess the extent to which they met their contractual obligations with their customers, their compliance with the relevant consumer protection regulation and their communication with customers in this area. Following this assessment:
    - lenders were required to calculate redress and compensation and implement a redress programme. The Central Bank also required lenders to set up an independent appeal process to deal with affected customers who were dissatisfied with any aspect of the redress and compensation offer they received from their lender.
    - the Central Bank successfully challenged lenders to include an additional 20 000 customer accounts within the scope of the Examination.
    - the Central Bank also judged the initial redress and compensation schemes proposed by some lenders to be materially deficient. It reviewed more than 30 iterations and had an estimated 220 engagements with lenders in relation to their proposed redress and compensation schemes, with a view to improving both the schemes and the appeals processes for the benefit of their customers.
    - between 2019 and 2022, the Central Bank reprimanded and fined 6 lenders for regulatory breaches affecting tracker mortgage customers.

Output for consumers

As of end of June 2023, lenders had identified around 42 000 affected customers and had paid out around EUR 744.5 million in redress and compensation.

Source: The Tracker Mortgage Examination - Final Report, Central Bank of Ireland (July 2019) (Central Bank of Ireland, 2019[85])

2.10. Principle 10: Protection of Consumer Assets against Fraud, Scams and Misuse

Principle 10 stipulates that oversight bodies and financial services providers should develop appropriate control and protection mechanisms for consumers' deposits, savings and other financial assets against fraud, scams, misappropriation and other misuses. These mechanisms should be adapted to new technologies and include clear and transparent liability arrangements between financial services providers and consumers in the event of financial loss. Oversight bodies should work together with relevant stakeholders to raise public awareness of digital security risks and promote safe online and digital transactions.

2.10.1. Role of the Central Bank and other public stakeholders relating to Principle 10

An Garda Síochána (Ireland's National Police and Security Service) investigates crimes of a fraudulent nature. The Central Bank is the competent authority for the supervision and enforcement of compliance with sectoral legislation requiring certain financial services firms to adopt strong customer authentication processes and to have measures in place to protect clients' assets and funds. The Central Bank also has a dedicated Unauthorised Providers Unit that investigates instances of alleged unauthorised activities. Members of the public can report such instances through the Central Bank's website.

The next paragraphs describe the provisions, the main trends and the activities of the Central Bank relating to Principle 10.

2.10.2. Standards and requirements

The PSR requires payment services firms to apply strong customer authentication when a consumer accesses payment accounts online, initiates an electronic payment or carries out any action remotely, and to refund customers in the event of unauthorised transactions on their account.

Moreover, payment and e-money institutions are required to have measures in place to safeguards clients' funds. The MiFID II Regulations require retail investment firms (and credit institutions providing MiFID investment services) to safeguard clients' financial instruments and assets. Finally, insurance and ancillary insurance intermediaries are required to protect their customers against the inability of the insurance intermediary to transfer the premium to the insurance undertaking or the amount of claim payable to the customer.

The Code currently requires firms to act honestly and professionally in their dealings with customers, and with due skill, care and diligence, and the proposals in the review of the Code include imposing a general Standard for Business on firms to control and manage their affairs and systems to counter the risks to customers of financial abuse, which is defined to cover all forms of frauds and scams as well as misappropriation and other misuses.

2.10.3. Protection of assets in the event of winding up or liquidation

Ireland has several schemes in place to protect consumers' financial assets in the event of winding up or liquidation. Retail banks and insurance companies are required to hold capital against their risks that can be used when unexpected losses occur. Where losses exceed the capital, the firm's resources are distributed to creditors and investors according to a hierarchy.

For retail banks, deposits covered by the Deposit Guarantee Scheme (DGS) rank in preference to unsecured creditors and equally with rates, taxes, wages and pension contributions. Uninsured deposits of natural persons and SMEs rank equally with unsecured creditors. The DGS protects deposits up to EUR 100 000 per person per institution. Where the funds in the DGS (which is approximately 0.8% of the covered deposits) are not sufficient to compensate eligible depositors, the DGS can raise additional contributions from credit institutions who are part of the scheme or can obtain urgent short-term funding from the Central Bank which is reclaimed from the Central Fund of the Exchequer.

For insurance companies, insurance claims have precedence over assets backing the technical provisions reserved for claims. Where the resources of the firm are not sufficient, the Insurance Compensation Fund (ICF) will pay compensation for claims on non-life insurance policies, up to the smaller of 65% of the claim or EUR 825 000, except for motor liability where 100% of the claim will be paid. In the case of motor liability, the ICF will recoup the amounts in excess of its normal limits from the Motor Insurance Insolvency Compensation Fund (MIICF), which was set up for the specific purpose of ensuring victims of motor accidents receive full compensation if a motor insurer becomes insolvent. The MIICF is maintained by the Motor Insurance Bureau of Ireland (MIBI).

The Central Bank's Client Asset Requirements oblige MiFID investment firms and credit institutions providing MiFID investment services to have measures in place to protect the assets belonging to the clients in case of the firm's insolvency (including, for example, holding clients' assets in a segregated account). In the event of the inability of a MiFID firm or a credit institution providing MiFID investment services to return the client's assets, compensation can be requested from the Investor Compensation Company DAC (ICCL) up to 90% of the amount lost subject to a maximum of EUR 20 000.

2.10.4. Co-ordination arrangements

The Central Bank is required to report to relevant bodies (such as *An Garda Síochána*) instances where the Central Bank suspects that a criminal offence may have been committed by a supervised entity. Moreover, the Central Bank participates in the Advisory Council against Economic Crime and Corruption and the Economic Crime and Corruption Forum together with a number of law enforcement agencies. These two bodies were recently established to enhance co-operation to combat corporate, economic and regulatory crime. The Central Bank will also support the work of the Anti-Fraud Forum, which was established under the Department of Finance's National Payments Strategy. The mandate of this forum relates specifically to payment fraud. A key focus of the forum is to improve co-ordination efforts between cross-sectoral stakeholders including financial institutions, telecommunication companies and social media companies.

2.10.5. Supervisory activity of the Central Bank

The top three categories of payment fraud in 2022 were related to card fraud, unauthorised electronic transfer fraud and unauthorised push payment fraud (Banking & Payments Federation Ireland, 2022[86]). The top three categories of scams reported to the Central Bank in relation to the unauthorised provision of financial services related to clone investment firms, where a fake website is created claiming to be a legitimate firm, to fraudulent firms contacting prospective clients about investment opportunities and using fake prospectus documents, and to unauthorised retail credit firms requesting advance fees.

The supervisory frameworks described in section 2.2.4 provide the structure for the Central Bank's supervisory approach with respect to protection of consumer assets against fraud, scams and misuse. An example of activities of the Central Bank relating to Principle 10 is its remediation work relating to one Irish bank's obligations under the PSR to implement strong customer authentication. Given the delay of one bank to implement the strong customer authentication standards outlined above, and following extensive engagement, the Central Bank took action against the bank and required that it could not charge a full fee to customers for a service that was not in full compliance with the relevant regulatory requirements. The bank was required to contact the affected customers and provide an explanation and apologise for the delay. As a result of this intervention the bank refunded around EUR 3 million to its customers. The Central

Bank also publishes warning notices and guidance to consumers to avoid scams (Central Bank of Ireland, 2023[87]).

2.11. Principle 11: Protection of Consumer Data and Privacy

Principle 11 promotes the safeguarding of consumer financial and personal information through effective control and protection measures. These measures should clearly outline the reasons for collecting, processing, storing, using and sharing data, particularly with third parties. Consumers' rights regarding consent for data sharing, access to their data, notification of data breaches, and avenues for redress, including timely correction or deletion of inaccuracy or unlawfully obtained data, should be recognised. Collaboration among oversight bodies responsible for consumer data protection and privacy is essential to ensure comprehensive protection.

2.11.1. Role of the Central Bank and other public stakeholders relating to Principle 11

The Data Protection Commission (DPC) is an independent body established under the Data Protection Act 2018. The DPC is responsible for upholding the right of individuals in Ireland to have their personal data protected and it supervises and enforces compliance with the Data Protection Legislation, which includes the General Data Protection Regulation (GDPR), the Data Protection Acts 1988 to 2018 and the Regulation on Privacy and Electronic Communications.

The Central Bank does not have a role in supervising compliance with the Data Protection Legislation. As a data controller, however, the Central Bank is subject to compliance with the Data Protection Legislation and the Central Bank has adopted policies, procedures and controls for this purpose.

When processing data, the Central Bank follows the GDPR principles of i) lawfulness, fairness and transparency, ii) purpose limitation, iii) data minimisation, iv) accuracy and v) integrity and confidentiality.

More broadly, the Central Bank's Information Security Policy (ISP) sets out information security requirements and guidance and it describes how records should be managed throughout their lifecycle, to support business and regulatory requirements and the historical legacy of the Central Bank.

Separate to Data Protection Legislation, the Central Bank is subject to a duty of confidentiality for information it holds on regulated firms and the exercise of its power/functions. The Central Bank Act 1942 sets out a number of gateways which may require or permit the Central Bank to disclose information in certain circumstances, including the requirement to report to other Irish authorities or to authorities carrying out a similar function (e.g. other European authorities or the European Central Bank) any information that leads the Central Bank to believe that a criminal offence may have been committed by a regulated firm, or that the regulated firm has breached a provision of certain legislation.

2.11.2. Co-ordination arrangements

As a data controller, the Central Bank is subject to the supervision of the DPC. There is no MOU or co-operation agreement in place between the DPC and the Central Bank. The Data Protection Legislation requires the Central Bank to consult with the DPC when the Central Bank is proposing to issue regulations which impact on the personal data of consumers.[6] In October 2022 the DPC responded to the discussion paper on the review of the Code to comment on the importance of avoiding conflicts between the Code and data protection legal requirements and fundamental rights of individuals (Data Protection Commission, 2022[88]). As part of the review of the Code, the Central Bank will consult with the DPC to ensure that such conflicts do not arise, and that any provisions requiring firms to process personal data is done in a way that reflects the principles of the Data Protection Legislation. The Central Bank may also engage with the DPC when it plans a material project impacting the collection of personal data from consumers.

2.12. Principle 12: Complaints Handling and Redress

Principle 12 stipulates that consumers, especially those in vulnerable circumstances, should have access to adequate complaints handling and redress mechanisms that are affordable, fair, independent, accountable, timely and efficient. Consistent with this, financial services providers and intermediaries should have mechanisms in place for consumer complaints handling and redress. Consumers should also have access to an independent redress process to handle complaints that are not resolved via firms' internal procedures. Aggregate information about consumer complaints should be made public.

2.12.1. Role of the Central Bank and other public stakeholders relating to Principle 12

The Central Bank is responsible for supervising and enforcing compliance with provisions requiring regulated firms to have complaints handling procedures in place. The Central Bank does not have a role in receiving, mediating or adjudicating on individual consumer complaints. However, the Central Bank conducts analysis of complaints data received from firms and the Financial Services and Pensions Ombudsman (see next paragraph) to inform its financial consumer protection supervisory function. The Central Bank has a Public Contact Unit (PCU) that responds to queries and information received from members of the public. Analysis of these queries informs the Central Bank's supervisory work.

The Financial Services and Pensions Ombudsman (FSPO) is an independent statutory body established in 2018 by the Financial Services and Pensions Ombudsman Act 2017 ("FSPO Act"). If a consumer, whether an individual, a small business or an organisation (with an annual turnover of less than €3 000 000) is unable to resolve a complaint or dispute with a financial service provider or a pension provider, they can refer their complaint to the FSPO. The FSPO provides an independent, impartial, fair and confidential service, which is free to consumers, to resolve complaints through either informal mediation, leading to a potential mediated settlement agreed between the parties, or formal investigation and adjudication, leading to a legally binding decision. Section 2.12.3 describes the FSPO's informal mediation and formal investigation processes in greater detail.

2.12.2. Internal dispute resolution procedures

The Code as well as sectoral legislation requires regulated firms to have complaints handling and redress procedures in place to handle consumer complaints. In addition, firms are required to clearly communicate information to consumers about their right to complain, to handle complaints speedily, efficiently and fairly, to report complaints data to the Central Bank and to ensure that the needs of consumers, including those experiencing vulnerability, are considered when designing and publicising complaints handling and redress procedures.

The Code also sets out specific timelines within which firms must attempt to resolve complaints, and timelines within which a firm must update consumers on the progress of the investigation until the complaint is resolved. Firms must also analyse patterns of complaints received from consumers on a regular basis, including investigating whether complaints indicate a more widespread issue for consumers. As part of the Central Bank's consultation on its review of the Code, the Central Bank is proposing to strengthen firms' governance obligations regarding complaints and to require firms to have systems in place to track and manage complaints. Firms will be obliged to analyse complaints on a regular basis and at least once every six months, in order to identify and address trends or other potential issues in a timely manner.

Firms are required to periodically submit to the Central Bank data on volumes of complaints that they have received from consumers and that have been referred to the FSPO. Insurance firms, credit institutions, retail credit firms, credit servicing firms and investment firms are also required to report information on the categories of complaints received. There are no requirements to make aggregated complaints data submitted by regulated firms to the Central Bank publicly available.

In 2023, based on data submitted by regulated firms to the Central Bank, the most frequent consumer complaints received by banks, retail credit firms and credit servicing firms relate to account administration and processing, customer service and provider policy, for example opening hours and daily limits,. For insurance firms, the most frequent consumer complaints relate to customer service, pricing and issues with the policy such as voiding or other terms and conditions. These two financial sectors were also those with the largest numbers of consumer complaints, and those that include the firms with the greatest number of customers and that provide the most important products and services. Finally, concerning MiFID investment firms the most frequent consumer complaints relate to customer service, problems with fees in managing investments and quality of, or lack of, information provided.

2.12.3. External dispute resolution mechanisms

The FSPO can resolve complaints through either informal mediation or formal investigation.

The Dispute Resolution Service (DRS) is a voluntary and confidential process through which the FSPO aims to help the complainant and their provider to themselves design and agree to a solution that satisfies both parties. The dispute resolution process typically takes 9 - 12 weeks. A mediation can have three potential outcomes: i) the complainant and the provider agree on a settlement, ii) the complainant receives clarification from the provider and closes the complaint and iii) no settlement is agreed, and the complaint proceeds to a formal investigation. In 2022 and 2023, 66% and 62% of complaints that were mediated reached a settlement, respectively.

When a complaint is not resolved by mediation, the formal investigation is carried out by the FSPO which gathers and examines all relevant evidence. In 2022, formal investigations typically took between 9 and 18 months, though more recently this timeline has increased, owing to the volume of complaints requiring formal investigation. At the start of the formal investigation, the FSPO issues a Summary of Complaint to the financial service provider or pension provider to request information and evidence, which may include documents and audio evidence. The Complainant is given the opportunity to comment on the response received from the provider, and information received from one party is shared with the other party, in accordance with the requirements of fair procedures. The sharing of observations and evidence continues until both parties have no further comments to make. The complaint will then proceed for adjudication.

In a small number of complaint investigations, the FSPO will decide that it is appropriate to hold an Oral Hearing, for the taking of testimony, and the cross examination of witnesses. This arises when there is a material conflict of fact in the evidence that cannot be resolved by reference to the documentary or audio evidence available. When the complaint has been fully investigated, the FSPO issues a preliminary decision to the parties. If both parties accept the preliminary decision, the FSPO issues a legally binding decision in the same terms, after 15 working days. Alternatively, during the 15 working days made available to the parties to consider the preliminary decision, either or both parties may indicate that they believe that the preliminary decision contains an error of fact or an error of law, or that they wish to offer additional evidence relevant to the contents of the preliminary decision. Upon receipt of such details, the parties' respective comments are shared with the other party, and the FSPO will reconsider the matter for adjudication in due course, taking into consideration the submissions made, and will then issue a legally binding decision.

A consumer can also issue legal proceedings against a financial service provider or pension provider. However, the FSPO is prohibited by statute from investigating a complaint where the issues arising are, or have been, the subject of court proceedings, except when the Court makes an Order pursuant to Section 49 of the FSPO Act, permitting the FSPO to proceed.

Table 2.3 shows the number of consumer complaints received by the FSPO in 2021, 2022 and 2023, broken down by sector. The total number of complaints received by the FSPO increased by 29% from 4 781 in 2022 to 6 182 in 2023. The sector with the largest number of complaints received by the FSPO is banking, which in 2023 represented 62% of complaints received. Insurance is the second largest sector (23% of complaints in 2023), with complaints about investments (7%) and pensions schemes (5%) much lower.

Table 2.3. Number of consumer complaints received by the FSPO by sector

Sector	Sub-sector	2021	2022	2023
Banking	Consumer credit	431	367	498
	Mortgages	1 081	814	1 150
	Retail and commercial banking	970	1 287	1 926
	Foreign Exchange	7	17	11
	Multiple banking products/ services	26	34	33
	Payments and e-money institutions	145	121	232
Insurance (general & life)		1 257	1 129	1 446
Retail investment products & services (including financial advice)		352	366	461
Pensions		186	233	336
Retail intermediaries		Reflected in the other categories		
Sector unconfirmed/unregulated		141	120	87
Unassigned at year end		62	293	2
Total		4 658	4 781	6 182

Source: Financial Services and Pensions Ombudsman (2024[89]), Overview of Complaints 2023, https://www.fspo.ie/documents/Overview-of-Complaints-2023.pdf

In 2023, the FSPO received 3 850 banking complaints, which represented an increase of 46% compared to the 2 640 banking complaints received in 2022. Banking complaints accounted for 62% of all complaints received by the FSPO. In 2023, the majority of banking complaints received by the FSPO concerned bank accounts, mortgages and consumer credit. The primary conduct driving these complaints was customer service. Customer service covers a range of issues such as communications, complaint handling, account access issues and the failure or delay in providing information. Disputed transactions and maladministration were the second and third most common categories of concern, respectively.

Insurance complaints accounted for 23% of all complaints received in 2023. The largest number of insurance complaints received related to motor insurance and private health insurance, and specifically with respect to claim handling and the rejection of a claim. The number of investment related complaints increased by 26% between 2022 and 2023, and the complaints received related mostly to maladministration, customer service and mis-selling (Financial Services and Pensions Ombudsman of Ireland, 2024[89]).

With respect to the conduct of pension providers, regulated by the Pensions Authority, the majority of complaints in 2023 related to occupational pension schemes, in particular suggested maladministration or dissatisfaction regarding the calculation of pension benefit.

In accordance with the Memorandum of Understanding between the FSPO and the Central Bank, statistical information about complaints-handling data is furnished by the FSPO to the Central Bank on an annual basis. It includes key complaint trends and details on complaints received by product and complaint type. The Central Bank and the FSPO meet regularly as part of ongoing engagement and information sharing arrangements. The FSPO is also required to make aggregate complaints data publicly available.

The FSPO publishes an annual Overview of Complaints during the first quarter of each year. It includes a summary of all complaints made to the FSPO during the previous year, a review of the trends and patterns in the making of complaints to the FSPO, a breakdown of the method by which the complaints made to the

FSPO were dealt with; and information about the outcomes of all complaints concluded or terminated (Financial Services and Pensions Ombudsman, 2024[90]). This annual publication also lists any legally binding decisions that have been formally referred by the FSPO to the Central Bank, the CCPC, or the Pensions Authority (the "regulatory authorities") with a view to promoting the consumer protection framework. Referrals take place for a variety of reasons including in circumstances where a complaint raises the possibility of a potentially systemic issue, which may warrant consideration by the regulatory authorities.

Finally, the FSPO is required to report to the Central Bank when it identifies a persistent pattern of complaints or facts or any other matter of concern for the Central Bank. The FSPO and the Central Bank can also share information with each other on a pro-active basis. The MoU between the Central Bank and the FSPO sets out the scope, level and various types of pro-active and continuous information exchange expected between both parties. Section 4 of the MoU covers meetings between the Central Bank and the FSPO at appropriate levels of seniority and the appointment of designated liaisons to ensure regular engagement, and section 5 of the MoU sets out the different types of information that the parties may exchange (Financial Services and Pensions Ombudsman, 2024[91]).

2.12.4. Use of complaints data

Analysis of data on complaints received by firms informs the Central Bank's financial consumer protection supervisory functions in several ways. For example, analysis of complaints data is used as an input in the annual SRAs as well as to inform firm-specific work, as unusually high levels of complaints related to a specific firm may be driven by certain practices. Therefore, complaints data is relevant to the Central Bank's supervisory activity in respect of many of the FCP Principles. The Central Bank also uses data on complaints received from the FSPO. As explained above, the FSPO may make a referral to the Central Bank when it observes a persistent pattern or matters that would concern the Central Bank. The Central Bank reviews each FSPO referral and takes action, as appropriate, in line with its mandate.

2.12.5. Supervisory activity of the Central Bank

The Central Bank conducts supervisory activities related to complaints handling and redress. For example, where the Central Bank has identified that a particular firm's poor complaints handling processes is a risk, it has undertaken a targeted review of the firm's complaints handling processes and issued an RMP setting out actions the firm must take to address the issue. This type of risk could be identified by the Central Bank through consideration of a number of factors, such as very low or very high complaints numbers reported versus peers, discrepancies in numbers of complaints reported to the Central Bank compared to the firm's internal governance fora, or indications that the firm's complaint handling procedures may not be in compliance with the provisions set out in the Code.

References

Banking & Payments Federation Ireland (2022), *Payment Fraud Report*, https://bpfi.ie/wp-content/uploads/2023/07/BPFI-Fraud-Report-H2-2022.pdf (accessed on 14 March 2024). [86]

Beere, B. et al. (2022), *The Great Account Migration: Lessons from Behavioural Economics (Beere, Byrne, Kelly and Pratap Singh)*. [78]

Byrne, S., K. Devine and Y. Mccarthy (2022), *Interrupting inertia, evidence from a mortgage refinancing field trial (Byrne, Devine and McCarthy)*. [74]

Central Bank of Ireland (2024), *Annual Report 2023 and Annual Performance Statement 2023-2024*. [20]

Central Bank of Ireland (2024), *Authorisation*, https://www.centralbank.ie/regulation/how-we-regulate/authorisation (accessed on 1 May 2024). [15]

Central Bank of Ireland (2024), *Authorisations and Gatekeeping Report Edition1*. [17]

Central Bank of Ireland (2024), *Central Bank of Ireland - The Commission*, https://www.centralbank.ie/about/who-we-are/the-commission (accessed on 11 March 2024). [19]

Central Bank of Ireland (2024), *Civil Society Roundtable*, https://www.centralbank.ie/events/event-detail/2023/12/06/default-calendar/civil-society-roundtable (accessed on 12 March 2024). [41]

Central Bank of Ireland (2024), *Consumer Hub*. [67]

Central Bank of Ireland (2024), *Consumer Protection Code Review - Consultation Paper*. [6]

Central Bank of Ireland (2024), *Consumer Research Bulletin - Marketing and Advertising of Investment Products*, https://www.centralbank.ie/docs/default-source/publications/consumer-protection-research/consumer-research-bulletin-marketing-and-advertising-investment-products.pdf?sfvrsn=44b1661a_5 (accessed on 6 November 2024). [26]

Central Bank of Ireland (2024), *Consumer Research Report - Pension and retirement income, key challenges for consumers*. [77]

Central Bank of Ireland (2024), *Dear CEO Letter - Thematic Review on Early Mortgage Arrears*. [51]

Central Bank of Ireland (2024), *Enforcement Actions*, https://www.centralbank.ie/news-media/legal-notices/enforcement-actions (accessed on 7 October 2024). [38]

Central Bank of Ireland (2024), *How We Make Policy*, https://www.centralbank.ie/regulation/how-we-regulate/policy/how-we-make-policy (accessed on 7 October 2024). [10]

Central Bank of Ireland (2024), *Mortgages and Financial Difficulty*, https://www.centralbank.ie/consumer-hub/mortgages-and-financial-difficulty (accessed on 8 October 2024). [52]

Central Bank of Ireland (2024), *Open & Engaged Charter*, https://www.centralbank.ie/about/open-engaged-charter (accessed on 4 September 2024). [44]

Central Bank of Ireland (2024), *Regulatory & Supervisory Outlook*, https://www.centralbank.ie/docs/default-source/publications/regulatory-and-supervisory-outlook-reports/regulatory-supervisory-outlook-report-2024.pdf?sfvrsn=e6b1621a_10 (accessed on 1 May 2024). [1]

Central Bank of Ireland (2024), "Regulatory Service Standards Performance Report: 2023". [16]

Central Bank of Ireland (2024), *Research Exchange*, https://www.centralbank.ie/research-exchange (accessed on 7 October 2024). [24]

Central Bank of Ireland (2023), *Annual report 2022 and Annual Performance Statement 2022-2023*. [37]

Central Bank of Ireland (2023), *Avoiding Scams and Unauthorised Activity*, https://www.centralbank.ie/regulation/how-we-regulate/authorisation/unauthorised-firms/avoiding-scams-and-unauthorised-activity (accessed on 14 March 2024). [87]

Central Bank of Ireland (2023), *Buy Now, Pay Later – do you know you are taking out a loan?*. [72]

Central Bank of Ireland (2023), *Central Bank warns on scam targeting consumers seeking cash loans*. [69]

Central Bank of Ireland (2023), *Code of Ethics*, http://www.centralbank.ie (accessed on 13 March 2024). [46]

Central Bank of Ireland (2023), *Consumer Protection Outlook Report 2023*. [60]

Central Bank of Ireland (2023), *Consumer Research Bulletin Buy Now Pay Later Consumer Insights Update*. [76]

Central Bank of Ireland (2023), *Credit Union News*. [14]

Central Bank of Ireland (2023), *Dear CEO Letter - MiFID Structured Retail Product Review – Supervisory Guidance*, http://www.centralbank.ie (accessed on 5 May 2024). [80]

Central Bank of Ireland (2023), *Dear CEO Letter - Re: 2021 Common Supervisory Action on the supervision of Costs and Fees of UCITS*, http://www.centralbank.ie (accessed on 2 May 2024). [28]

Central Bank of Ireland (2023), *Dear CEO letter - Re: 2022 ESMA Common Supervisory Action on Asset Valuation*, http://www.centralbank.ie (accessed on 3 May 2024). [34]

Central Bank of Ireland (2023), *Dear CEO Letter - Re: Common Supervisory Action on MiFID II Costs and Charges Requirements*, http://www.centralbank.ie (accessed on 3 May 2024). [25]

Central Bank of Ireland (2023), *Dear CEO Letter - Re: Supervisory Findings and Expectations for Payment and Electronic Money (E-Money) Firms*, http://www.centralbank.ie (accessed on 2 May 2024). [27]

Central Bank of Ireland (2023), *Dear CEO Letter - Re: Thematic Review on the Ongoing Suitability of Long-Term Life Assurance Products*, http://www.centralbank.ie (accessed on 3 May 2024). [32]

Central Bank of Ireland (2023), *Dear CEO Letter - Targeted Reviews on Control Frameworks and Risk Appetite Statements in MiFID 1 Investment*, http://www.centralbank.ie (accessed on 3 May 2024). [29]

Central Bank of Ireland (2023), *Explainer – How can I protect myself from financial scams?*. [70]

Central Bank of Ireland (2023), *Guidance on Fitness and Probity Standards*. [83]

Central Bank of Ireland (2023), *Insurance Newsletter*. [31]

Central Bank of Ireland (2023), *Insurance Quarterly News*. [13]

Central Bank of Ireland (2023), *Intermediary Times Newsletters*, https://www.centralbank.ie/regulation/industry-market-sectors/brokers-retail-intermediaries/newsletters (accessed on 1 May 2024). [12]

Central Bank of Ireland (2023), *Overview of Account Migration Activity & Final Statistics 1. Overview.* [55]

Central Bank of Ireland (2023), *Protecting consumers in a changing economic landscape.* [30]

Central Bank of Ireland (2023), *Quarterly Bulletin - September 2023*, https://www.centralbank.ie/docs/default-source/publications/quarterly-bulletins/qb-archive/2023/quarterly-bulletin-q3-2023.pdf?sfvrsn=2dc49c1d_5 (accessed on 5 May 2024). [48]

Central Bank of Ireland (2023), *Retail Intermediary Roadshow*, https://www.centralbank.ie/regulation/industry-market-sectors/brokers-retail-intermediaries/retail-intermediary-roadshow (accessed on 13 March 2024). [43]

Central Bank of Ireland (2023), *Review of Differential Pricing Regulations in the Private Car and Home Insurance Markets.* [75]

Central Bank of Ireland (2023), *Thematic Review on the Ongoing Suitability of Long-Term Life Assurance Products*, http://www.centralbank.ie (accessed on 15 March 2024). [84]

Central Bank of Ireland (2022), *Campaign on short-term credit.* [50]

Central Bank of Ireland (2022), *Central Bank review identifies evidence of increasing levels of under-insurance in the home insurance market*, https://www.centralbank.ie/news-media/press-releases/central-bank-review-identifies-evidence-of-increasing-levels-of-under-insurance-in-the-home-insurance-market (accessed on 13 March 2024). [79]

Central Bank of Ireland (2022), *Central Bank warning on investing in crypto-assets.* [68]

Central Bank of Ireland (2022), *Consumer Protection Code Review - Discussion Paper*, https://www.centralbank.ie/docs/default-source/regulation/consumer-protection/other-codes-of-conduct/consumer-protection-code-review/consumer-protection-code-review-discussion-paper.pdf (accessed on 10 March 2024). [5]

Central Bank of Ireland (2022), *Dear CEO - Withdrawal of retail banks from the Irish market*, http://www.centralbank.ie (accessed on 1 May 2024). [57]

Central Bank of Ireland (2022), *Dear CEO Letter - e: Protecting consumers in a Changing Economic Landscape*, http://www.centralbank.ie (accessed on 5 May 2024). [49]

Central Bank of Ireland (2022), *Dear CEO letter - MiFID Structured Retail Product Review*, http://www.centralbank.ie (accessed on 8 March 2024). [36]

Central Bank of Ireland (2022), *How can I make my savings work harder?*, https://www.centralbank.ie/consumer-hub/saving-your-money (accessed on 5 May 2024). [71]

Central Bank of Ireland (2022), *Innovation Hub - 2022 Update*, http://www.centralbank.ie/regulation/innovation-hub (accessed on 13 March 2024). [45]

Central Bank of Ireland (2022), *Perspectives on the Evolution of Retail Banking in Ireland Central Bank Response to the Retail Banking Review Public Consultation Contents.* [18]

Central Bank of Ireland (2022), *Quarterly Bulletin - October 2022*, https://www.centralbank.ie/docs/default-source/publications/quarterly-bulletins/qb-archive/2022/quarterly-bulletin-q4-2022.pdf?sfvrsn=1666951d_6 (accessed on 5 May 2024). [47]

Central Bank of Ireland (2022), *Remarks by Director of Consumer Protection Colm Kincaid at Compliance Institute Annual Conference*, https://www.centralbank.ie/news/article/remarks-by-director-of-consumer-protection-colm-kincaid-at-compliance-institute-annual-conference (accessed on 2 May 2024). [22]

Central Bank of Ireland (2022), *The Central Bank's framework for the macroprudential mortgage measures*. [42]

Central Bank of Ireland (2022), *Understanding Repayment Amounts of Long-Term Mortgage Arrears Borrowers*. [58]

Central Bank of Ireland (2021), *Consultation Paper 136 - Enhancing our Engagement with Stakeholders*. [39]

Central Bank of Ireland (2021), *Consumer Protection Code 2012 - Guidance*. [11]

Central Bank of Ireland (2021), *Consumer Protection Code 2021 - updated May 2021*. [4]

Central Bank of Ireland (2021), *Consumer protection expectations in a changing retail banking landscape 2021*, http://www.centralbank.ie (accessed on 9 March 2024). [56]

Central Bank of Ireland (2021), *Cross-Industry Guidance on Outsourcing*, http://www.centralbank.ie (accessed on 15 March 2024). [81]

Central Bank of Ireland (2021), *Our Strategy*. [40]

Central Bank of Ireland (2021), *Regulatory Requirements and Guidance for High Cost Credit Providers*, https://www.centralbank.ie/regulation/industry-market-sectors/high-cost-credit-providers/regulatory-requirements-and-guidance (accessed on 15 March 2024). [2]

Central Bank of Ireland (2021), *Review of Differential Pricing in the Private Car and Home Insurance Markets*. [33]

Central Bank of Ireland (2020), *COVID-19 and Business Interruption Insurance Supervisory Framework*. [35]

Central Bank of Ireland (2019), *The Tracker Mortgage Examination Final Report*, http://www.centralbank.ie (accessed on 10 March 2024). [85]

Central Bank of Ireland (2018), *Addendum to the Consumer Protection 2012 - June 2018*. [73]

Central Bank of Ireland (2018), *Behaviour and Culture of the Irish Retail Banks*. [82]

Central Bank of Ireland (2017), *A Guide to Consumer Protection Risk Assessment*. [21]

Central Bank of Ireland (2017), *Minimum Competency Code*. [9]

Central Bank of Ireland (2016), *Code of Conduct on the Switching of Payment Accounts with Payment Service Providers*. [8]

Central Bank of Ireland (2013), *Code of Conduct on Mortgage Arrears*. [7]

Central Bank of Ireland (2013), *Unofficial Consolidation of the Consumer Protection Code 2012*. [3]

Competition and Consumer Protection Commission (2023), *Financial Wellbeing in Ireland: Financial literacy and inclusion in 2023*, https://www.indecon.ie/assets/files/pdf/financial_wellbeing_in_ireland_-_report_on_financial_literacy_and_inclusion_2023.pdf (accessed on 9 March 2024). [66]

Competition and Consumer Protection Commission (2023), *Online Behaviour - Influencer Marketing*, https://www.ccpc.ie/business/wp-content/uploads/sites/3/2022/12/2022.12.12-172837-CCPC-Influencer-marketing-report.pdf (accessed on 9 March 2024). [65]

Competition and Consumer Protection Commission (2022), *Pensions Research*, https://www.ccpc.ie/business/wp-content/uploads/sites/3/2022/09/CCPC-Pensions-Research-2022.pdf (accessed on 9 March 2024). [63]

Data Protection Commission (2022), *Response of the DPC to the discussion paper on the review of the Central Bank Consumer Protection Code*, https://www.centralbank.ie/docs/default-source/publications/discussion-papers/discussion-paper-10/data-protection-commission---response-to-dp10.pdf?sfvrsn=be339f1d_2 (accessed on 13 March 2024). [88]

Department of Finance (2024), *Financial Literacy in Ireland: Evidence Base for a National Strategy*, https://www.gov.ie/pdf/?file=https://assets.gov.ie/290810/16ca8875-42db-468e-9c80-efc4c45382e8.pdf#page=null (accessed on 27 June 2024). [62]

Department of Finance (2024), *Minister McGrath secures Government approval for Access to Cash legislation*, https://www.gov.ie/en/press-release/43af7-minister-mcgrath-secures-government-approval-for-access-to-cash-legislation/ (accessed on 17 February 2024). [54]

Department of Finance (2023), *National Financial Literacy Strategy*. [61]

Department of Finance (2022), *Retail Banking Review*, https://www.gov.ie/pdf/?file=https://assets.gov.ie/240770/d8b98fef-fe6a-4df8-b7d6-2f63e9f224b8.pdf#page=null (accessed on 17 February 2024). [53]

Financial Services and Pensions Ombudsman (2024), *Memorandum of Understanding (MOU)*, https://www.fspo.ie/governance/mou.asp. [91]

Financial Services and Pensions Ombudsman (2024), *Overview of Complaints*, http://www.fspo.ie/decisions (accessed on 14 March 2024). [90]

Financial Services and Pensions Ombudsman of Ireland (2024), *Overview of Complaints 2023*. [89]

Gaffney, E. and P. Lyons (2024), *An overview of the consumer credit market in Ireland*. [23]

Kelly, J. et al. (2021), *Long-term mortgage arrears: Analytical evidence for policy considerations*, https://www.centralbank.ie/docs/default- (accessed on 9 March 2024). [59]

Timmons, S., D. Robertson and P. Lunn (2022), "Combining nudges and boosts to increase precautionary saving: A large-scale field experiment". [64]

Notes

[1] These criteria include i) the promotion of fair competition between credit institutions, and credit institutions carrying on a particular type of banking or financial business, ii) the statement of commercial justification provided by the firm iii) a credit institution passing any costs on to its customers or a group of its customers in proposing to impose or change any charge, in relation to the provision of a service to a customer or a group of its customers, and iv) the effect on customers or a group of customers of any proposal to impose or change any charge in relation to the provision of such service.

[2] From a prudential perspective, the European Central Bank (ECB) is the competent authority for the supervision of significant institutions in the euro area, while less significant institutions are supervised by national competent authorities like the Central Bank.

[3] This applies where the Central Bank makes Regulations under either section 17A of Central Bank Reform Act 2010, or section 48 of the Central Bank (Supervision and Enforcement) Act 2013.

[4] The Markets in Crypto-Assets Regulation (MiCAR) became applicable for issuers of asset reference tokens and issuers of e-money tokens on 30 June 2024. MiCAR will become applicable for issuers of utility tokens and crypto-asset service providers on 30 December 2024.

[5] Age Action, Alone, Ask About Money, FLAC, Focus Ireland, ICTU, Irish Council for Social Housing, Irish Mortgage Holders Association, National Travellers MABS, Protestant Aid, Simon Communities, Social Justice Ireland and Threshold.

[6] For example, during the Discussion Paper phase of the Code review, the Central Bank met bilaterally with the Data Protection Commission (DPC) on one occasion, and the DPC attended the Central Bank's joint industry/civil society roundtable discussion on the theme 'Availability & Choice'. The DPC also made a formal submission in response to the Discussion Paper on the Code.

3 Assessment of the financial consumer protection supervisory functions of the Central Bank of Ireland and recommendations

This chapter presents the assessment of the financial consumer protection supervisory functions of the Central Bank. The chapter draws on the detailed mapping set out in Chapter 2 as well as international experience and interviews with representatives of the Central Bank and other relevant Irish institutions to identify areas for improvements. For each area, the chapter describes the relevant practices of the Central Bank and the OECD recommendations.

The financial consumer protection supervisory functions of the Central Bank align closely with the FCP Principles, and they play a crucial role in overseeing Ireland's financial markets and ensuring their proper functioning by promoting transparency, fairness and trust within the financial sector. The Central Bank has appropriate policies and practices in place to effectively monitor financial markets, identify risks to consumers and improve outcomes for consumers. The Central Bank plays a central role in Ireland's financial consumer protection landscape and has mechanisms in place to effectively co-operate with other relevant stakeholders where appropriate.

The review focusses on the financial consumer protection supervisory functions of the Central Bank and in keeping with its scope (see section 1.3), the identified recommendations:

- are addressed to the Central Bank (and not other stakeholders)
- focus on the financial consumer protection supervisory functions of the Central Bank (and do not cover its other functions)
- acknowledge the characteristics of Ireland's retail financial services and of the Central Bank's financial consumer protection supervisory functions
- provide sufficient details to allow the Central Bank to ensure that they can be implemented, while allowing the Central Bank to choose how to implement them
- are based on best practices in other jurisdictions to ensure they are practical in nature
- are achievable in the medium term.

Based on the detailed mapping set out in Chapter 2, interviews with representatives of the Central Bank and other relevant Irish institutions and international experiences, this chapter sets out the areas for improvement identified by the review. For each theme, the chapter describes the relevant practices of the Central Bank and the OECD recommendations.

The recommendations cover six themes:

- Theme 1 – Ensuring consumers continue to be protected as part of the Central Bank's integrated supervisory approach
- Theme 2 – Measuring and demonstrating the effectiveness of the financial consumer protection supervisory functions of the Central Bank
- Theme 3 – Engaging with consumer and consumer groups
- Theme 4 – Informing and educating financial consumers
- Theme 5 – Protecting consumers experiencing vulnerability
- Theme 6 – Using data in financial consumer protection supervision.

3.1. Theme 1 – Ensuring consumers continue to be protected as part of the Central Bank's integrated supervisory approach

Retail conduct supervision is an essential component of financial regulation and aims to ensure that financial services providers and other market participants operate fairly, transparently and efficiently. It plays a crucial role in maintaining the integrity and stability of financial systems by overseeing the behaviour of market participants and enforcing rules and standards. It encompasses various activities to identify, monitor, prevent and mitigate market conduct risks including the risk of misconduct, with the ultimate goals of protecting consumers, fostering trust and ensuring fair competition.

The review of the financial consumer protection supervisory functions of the Central Bank was based on the supervisory framework in operation at the time of the review. In its 2021 Strategic Plan, the Central Bank committed to transforming its approach to supervision so that it is better positioned to meet its objectives to ensure consumers of financial services are protected in all respects in a changing and increasingly complex and interconnected financial landscape (Central Bank of Ireland, 2021[1]).

As set out in section 2.2.4, the Central Bank is evolving its framework to deliver a more integrated approach to supervision, across its overall mandate, and complemented by a revised operating structure. The recommendations in this report are intended to support the Central Bank's transformation and touch on some of the areas of strategic focus for the Central Bank, including accelerating the evolution of its risk-based supervisory approach. Delivered in conjunction with an integrated supervisory approach, the recommendations represent an opportunity for the Central Bank to drive ever better outcomes for consumers.

Recommendation

In evolving its framework to deliver a more integrated supervisory approach, the Central Bank should ensure that its governance and supervisory structures retain explicit consumer and investor protection objectives, to make retail financial markets deliver good outcomes for consumers.

3.2. Theme 2 – Measuring and demonstrating the effectiveness of the financial consumer protection supervisory functions of the Central Bank (Principle 2)

Measuring and demonstrating the effectiveness of its activity is crucial for an oversight body. It enables a better understanding of what interventions work most effectively by identifying strengths and weaknesses in the approach used as well as opportunities for improvement. Once mechanisms to measure and demonstrate effectiveness become fully embedded, they can increase transparency in the authority's decision-making process over time and can be used to enhance accountability.

The main objectives of measuring the effects of supervisory activity are to enable supervisors to determine whether intended outcomes of an intervention have been achieved and to increase supervisors' understanding of what interventions are effective. Over time, it can also show relevant stakeholders the value added by supervisors' activity, increasing transparency, accountability, and trust in the supervisory activity.

The financial consumer protection supervisory functions of the Central Bank are well aligned with Principle 2 which states that oversight bodies should regularly assess the effectiveness of supervisory tools. There are number of ways in which the Central Bank embeds effectiveness checks in relation to its consumer protection supervisory functions in its ways of working. For example:

- the Central Bank's Supervisory Risk Committee (SRC) advises on issues central to the management of supervisory risks and on the development and enhancement of risk-based supervision and supervisory engagement (see section 2.2.4).
- the Sector Strategy Governance Panels (SSGPs) assess the appropriateness of the proposed supervisory strategy and supervisory engagement plan for a particular sector in treating identified risks as well as the effectiveness of the previous strategy in delivering the desired consumer outcomes (see section 2.2.4).
- the Central Bank's Supervisory Quality Assurance assesses, using a risk-based approach, whether reasonable assurance can be given that the quality and depth of supervisory engagement has been effective in identifying and mitigating key risks and achieving outcome-focused supervision.

- the Central Bank's Internal Audit systematically evaluates the effectiveness of the Central Bank's risk management, control and governance processes, including in relation to the Central Bank's supervisory functions (Central Bank of Ireland, 2024[2]).
- the Central Bank's Guidance on Consumer Protection Risk Assessment sets out the expectation on firms' risk management frameworks, including firm monitoring to ensure that fair outcomes are being achieved.
- when seeking to enhance its approach in a particular area, the Central Bank may seek to learn from other leading consumer protection authorities, either through bilateral engagements, or by carrying out research to identify whether more effective approaches are possible in relation to a particular aspect of its role (see section 2.2.11).
- the Central Bank is subject to peer reviews by the European Supervisory Authorities, which seek to strengthen consistency in supervisory outcomes across the EU.
- as part of delivering its Strategy, the Central Bank has undertaken a review of its approach to supervision, seeking to ensure its approach remains risk based, effective and agile in the context of an evolving financial system. Supervision in this regard refers to the full life cycle of financial services providers from authorisation to ongoing supervision to revocation/resolution and including enforcement action.
- the Central Bank conducts work to assess the impact of its supervisory activity. For example, as described in section 2.6.4, in December 2023 the Central Bank published a report on the impact of the ban of price walking in the home and motor insurance markets, finding that consumers who remain with their current provider are no longer paying a loyalty penalty (Central Bank of Ireland, 2023[3]).

While the Central Bank embeds a number of effectiveness checks in relation to its consumer protection supervisory functions in its ways of working and has in the past assessed the impact of its supervisory activity on an ad-hoc basis (e.g. on the assessment of the introduction of the ban of price walking described above), the Central Bank could evolve its supervisory framework by embedding an approach to assess the impact on consumer outcomes of its financial consumer protection functions, as part of its risk assessment and prioritisation process.

Moreover, some industry representatives interviewed by the OECD discussed the use by the Central Bank of "Dear CEO" letters. "Dear CEO" letters are a flexible tool that allow the Central Bank to quickly communicate changes to all financial services providers in a sector, including in a changing landscape, or that can be used to highlight both good and bad practices to all financial services providers within a sector following a thematic review of a sample of providers. However, while some industry representatives interviewed by the OECD noted the usefulness of "Dear CEO" letters in clarifying the Central Bank's expectations, others have stated that "Dear CEO" letters have become more frequent, covering more topics at once, which increases the burden especially for smaller financial services providers.

Recommendations

The Central Bank should:

- Build on existing initiatives to embed the evaluation of the effectiveness of its financial consumer protection supervisory activities on consumer outcomes in its supervisory framework.
- Assess and review the effectiveness of "Dear CEO" letters as a supervisory tool.

3.2.1. International experience

Measuring the impact of supervision is an emerging priority for financial oversight bodies (Bank for International Settlements, 2015[4]). Different jurisdictions have implemented a range of practices to demonstrate how their activities (including retail conduct supervision) contribute to the overall health of the financial system and several authorities have frameworks in place to assess the impact of their activity on consumer outcomes. However, conducting such analysis is not without complexities, as oversight bodies face significant methodological challenges, and no single method or indicator can be used to address these challenges. This section provides examples from selected jurisdictions to provide points of comparison.

Measuring the impact of supervision is considered an integral part of the supervisory process by the *Autoriteit Financiële Markten* (AFM), Netherlands' financial oversight body, and the *De Nederlandsche Bank* (DNB), Netherlands' central bank (Hilbers et al., 2013[5]).In 2024 the UK Financial Conduct Authority (FCA), the UK's market conduct oversight body, published a Rule Review Framework (Framework) describing how the FCA sets, measures and monitors the outcomes of its rules or interventions (Financial Conduct Authority, 2024[6]).

Challenges when measuring effectiveness of supervisory activity

Hilbers et al. (2013[5]), the Bank of International Settlements (2015[4]) and FCA (2024[6]) identify the most common challenges relating to measuring the effectiveness of supervisory actions. These include identifying and isolating the causal effect of interventions, communicating to the public the effects of interventions that may be aimed at individual institutions and may not be in the public domain, considering an appropriate time horizon to assess impact, focussing on certain performance metrics and, finally, ensuring the availability of resources to conduct such assessments. These challenges are described below.

- One of the most significant challenges in evaluating supervisory performance lies in demonstrating a clear and direct relationship between supervisory activity and the resulting outcomes. This difficulty arises in part from the need to find a reliable counterfactual scenario of what would have happened in the absence of the intervention or a control group against which to measure the impact of the intervention taking into account external factors and controlling for the changing market environment. Furthermore, the nature of risk-based supervision adds another layer of complexity. Since this approach focusses on areas and institutions where risks are most pronounced, there is an inherent selection bias. Institutions under the strictest supervision may be those already facing significant challenges, which may lead to worse outcomes. Therefore, the difficulty in assessing supervisory effectiveness is compounded by the challenge of separating the influence of supervision from the broader context in which it operates.
- Another challenge is represented by confidentiality requirements that may make it difficult for oversight bodies to communicate and demonstrate the effectiveness of their activity, as often oversight bodies face limitations in the amount of information that can be publicly disclosed about individual financial services providers.
- Defining the time horizon poses another significant challenge when evaluating the impact of supervisory activities. Supervisory interventions may take a significant time to produce a visible effect, but the longer the time between intervention and evaluation, the more market conditions may change and make it harder to establish a causal relationship.
- Identifying and focussing on certain performance metrics can create perverse incentives by focussing supervisory attention on that specific metric, diverting resources from activities that are measured less easily or less frequently. For example, the existence of a simple indicator based on the number of supervisory interventions may increase the number of interventions, but it may not necessarily help in addressing the underlying risk.

- Finally, reliable measures of the effects of supervisory intervention typically require significant amount of resources. To obtain credible estimates of the effects of supervisory activity there is typically a need to develop a robust methodology, collect ad-hoc data from financial services providers and ensure adequate expertise is available, either in-house or externally (for example from consultants or academics expert in evaluation techniques). Given the limited resources available, measuring the effectiveness should be explicitly incorporated in the supervisory process and the interventions whose effects are evaluated should be selected based on transparent criteria (e.g. based on the novelty of the approach or the significance of the intervention).

Ways to address these challenges

While the challenges described above may increase the uncertainty of the measurements and the costs incurred to obtaining them, there are practical steps that can be taken to obtain reasonable estimates of the effects of supervision.

(Hilbers et al., 2013[5]) argues that oversight bodies can increase the plausibility of the measurements by identifying more specific objectives of a supervisory intervention at a "micro level". This can make it easier to draw a causal link between intervention and objectives and to measure the effects of the intervention. The example used by (Hilbers et al., 2013[5]) is the supervisory activity to protect retail investment from high-risk, complex investment products. An indicator of the effectiveness of such supervisory activity could be a measurement of the capital inflows from retail investors, as lower capital inflows (potentially compared to capital inflows of similar products, to attempt controlling for market conditions) could mean that the supervisory activity is achieving its objectives.

Another way to obtain a reasonable estimate is to develop a plausible theory of change to link the intervention to the observed outcome. This is sometimes called "contribution analysis" (Mayne, 2012[7]). A tool to build such a theory of change is a results chain or a logic chart, which distinguishes between effort indicators, such as the resources used and the supervisory intervention, and effect indicators, such as the output of the intervention (e.g. the number of individual firms subject to the supervisory activity), the compliance effect (i.e. the increase compliance with a standard or regulation) and the societal effects (i.e. an improvement of outcomes for consumers).

Finally, (Hilbers et al., 2013[5]) argues for the need of having a range of indicators to measure the impact of supervisory activity. This is important because a portfolio of indicators may better capture complex objectives such as those of supervisory activity. A range of indicators may also be less sensitive to the challenges highlighted above compared to a single indicator. Consistent with this, the framework designed by the FCA (Financial Conduct Authority, 2024[6]) describes three main types of reviews that the FCA can undertake, depending on the nature of the intervention: i) evidence assessment, ii) post-implementation review and iii) impact evaluation.

- an *evidence assessment* is designed to be a low resource intensive process, suitable where a less in-depth review is sufficient to assess if the intervention has achieved its intended outcomes, and whether there have been market developments that may have affected the effectiveness of the intervention.
- *a post-implementation review* seeks to assess whether the intervention i) was implemented as intended, ii) has achieved its objectives, iii) has caused unintended consequences, and iv) whether there were obstacles to its implementation.
- finally, the FCA conducts *impact evaluations* to identify, isolate and quantify the causal effect of discrete interventions on consumer outcomes and to estimate their costs and benefits. (Financial Conduct Authority, 2024[8]) describes the methodological approaches that can be used.

Other approaches

Some authorities have trialled a customer outcomes-based approach, whereby rather than just complying with rules and regulations, regulated financial services providers are required to monitor consumer outcomes when using their products. One example is the pilot study conducted by the Financial Sector Conduct Authority (FSCA), South Africa's financial services regulator (CGAP, 2022[9]). As part of the pilot, the FSCA identified, in collaboration with the financial industry, a range of indicators of consumer outcomes, and required financial services providers to monitor such indicators and submit regular data to the FSCA.

3.3. Theme 3 – Engaging with consumers and consumer groups (Principle 2)

Financial oversight bodies have a range of ways to engage with consumers. For example, oversight bodies can solicit feedback from the public and consumer advocacy groups on prospective rules and regulations, establish committees to provide regular input on market and/or regulatory development, conduct surveys to gather data on consumer experiences, needs and attitudes towards financial products and services, and monitor complaints and social media. These activities are important to improve understanding of the needs of consumers, identify potential issues early, improve decision-making process, increase transparency, and build trust in the regulatory and supervisory process. The FCP Principles underscore the importance of engagement with relevant stakeholders and engagement with stakeholders is discussed under Principle 2 on the role of oversight bodies. This section discusses engagement with consumers and consumer groups and small businesses in their capacity as consumers of financial services.

Consistent with Principle 2, the Central Bank has a range of mechanisms in place to engage with stakeholders, including consumers or entities that can provide an insight into the consumer experience and small businesses, that align well with the FCP Principles. Ensuring the involvement of these groups is crucial for creating effective and equitable financial consumer protection policies and practices, and the Central Bank works to provide them with necessary resources, information and opportunities to participate meaningfully in discussions and decision-making processes and ensure that the perspective and needs of consumers are adequately represented and addressed. For example, in July 2024, the Central Bank published an "Open and Engaged" Charter setting out its approach to stakeholder engagement (Central Bank of Ireland, 2024[10]). This reflects the Central Bank's ambition to expand its reach and impact by building relationships with a wider range of stakeholders, including the public and participants in the real economy. The recommendations in this section may support the Central Bank to achieve this ambition.

As set out in section 2.2.11, the Central Bank has mechanisms in place to engage with consumers and consumer representatives, such as public consultations, regular meetings with the Consumer Advisory Group (CAG), roundtables with civil society organisations and regular engagement with consumer associations about risk drivers identified in the Central Bank's Outlook Reports. Challenges faced by and risks to consumers are also raised with the Central Bank via public contacts (section 2.2.4), protected disclosures (section 2.2.9), media queries and Parliamentary Questions (section 2.2.1) and may also be identified through the Central Bank's social media monitoring (section 2.2.11).

However, interviews with the Central Bank and other stakeholders suggested that it may be challenging for the Central Bank to obtain the consumer perspective on the broad range of financial consumer protection matters within its remit. Therefore, it is important that the Central Bank continues to innovate in how it engages consumers.

The CAG is a valuable source of expertise and provides helpful feedback on the activity of the Central Bank to protect consumers in financial markets. As set out in section 2.2.11, the Central Bank consults the CAG about its multi-year Sectoral Strategies, which set out sectoral priorities, desired outcomes and high-level activities to address sectoral risks. This provides the CAG with an explicit opportunity to raise with the Central Bank any additional risks that CAG members may be aware of. In addition, the Central Bank presents to the CAG the risks identified from the Sectoral Risk Assessment (SRA) process each year. However, the CAG is not a source of structured data on emerging risks to consumers.

Currently, the CAG includes members that can provide a perspective on the Irish consumer landscape, such as the representatives of MABS and Social Justice Ireland, as well as a former Chair of the CCPC and current Chair of Safeguarding Ireland. The Central Bank also has mechanisms in place to support and facilitate the work of CAG members. The Central Bank also makes available to CAG members a Secretariat that proactively engages with members and the Chair to set out an annual plan of activity and a forward-looking agenda of issues. CAG agenda is driven by CAG members, with a focus on informed discussions on identified issues. Central Bank experts on the topics attend meetings and are available to discuss with the CAG members.

The Central Bank has mechanisms in place to engage with small businesses that are consumers of financial services where appropriate, including recently in the context of the consolidation in the retail banking market (see section 2.2.11).

Finally, while the Central Bank carries out consumer research, the Central Bank does not conduct periodic surveys of adults' financial behaviour and experiences of financial services. As described in section 3.3.1, such surveys could be a valuable source of data on emerging risks to consumers.

Recommendations

The Central Bank should:

- Enhance the Consumer Advisory Group (CAG) to ensure that it includes the consumer perspective on the broad range of financial consumer protection matters within the remit of the Central Bank. This could be done, for example, by reserving some space on the CAG for representatives of consumers or consumer associations. This would build on the valuable role that the CAG already plays in advising the Central Bank and would help the CAG to provide a broader view of the Irish consumer experience.
- Conduct periodic surveys of Ireland's adult population to evaluate and track consumer behaviours and attitudes towards financial products and services and to build consumer segmentation models.
- Conduct more regular engagement with small businesses in their capacity as consumers of financial services. This could be done, for example, by including representatives of small businesses in the current structure for consumer engagement.

3.3.1. International experience

The Central Bank's practices to engage with consumers and small businesses are broadly aligned with the practices of other oversight bodies. This section provides examples on the use of consumer advisory panels and surveys of financial consumers' attitudes and behaviour from selected financial consumer protection oversight bodies.

Consumer Advisory Panels

Consumer advisory panels can be an effective way of capturing the perspective of consumers and facilitating the early identification of risks for consumers (Newbury and Duflos, 2022[11]). Such panels have been established to advise financial oversight bodies in many jurisdictions. For example, in the United Kingdom, the Financial Services Consumer Panel (Consumer Panel) provides advice and challenge to the

FCA in relation to its statutory duties and its consumer protection objective. The Consumer Panel is independent and represents the interests of consumers of financial services (including small businesses). Members of the Consumer Panel are recruited through a process of open competition and currently include individuals with experience of consumer advice, campaigning, communications, market research, journalism, law, the financial services industry, financial inclusion, financial regulation and compliance, and later life issues. The FCA Board agrees a Budget for Panel members' fees, expenses and any consultancy or research work it commissions. The Panel is supported by a Secretariat of 5 FTE staff.

The United States' Consumer Financial Protection Bureau (CFPB) has established several advisory committees for different purposes. Two of these committees advise the CFPB on consumer matters:

- the Consumer Advisory Board includes experts, industry representatives, consumers, community leaders, consumer advocates and representatives of underserved communities. The Consumer Advisory Board is a source of intelligence and advises the CFPB on the impact of emerging products, practices, or services on consumers and other market participants (Consumer Financial Protection Bureau, 2024[12])
- the Academic Research Council is composed of economic experts and academics with strong research or practitioner background and a record of involvement in research and public policy. The committee advises the CFPB on its research agenda and provides feedback on research methodologies, data collection strategies, and methods of analysis (Consumer Financial Protection Bureau, 2024[13]).

The Australian Securities and Investments Commission (ASIC) established the ASIC Consumer Consultative Panel (ACCP) in 1998. The objectives of the ACCP are to provide insight on emerging consumer issues in financial services, to provide feedback on proposed regulatory changes and to inform the development and delivery of ASIC's strategic and operational objectives. ASIC remunerates members and the Chairs of the ACCP by paying a sitting fee for each full day meeting and covers any reasonable travel costs for each full day meeting attended in person (Australia Securities and Investment Commission, 2024[14]).

Survey of consumers' financial behaviour, experiences and attitudes

Several oversight bodies conduct periodic surveys of adults' financial behaviour and experiences of financial services. The objectives of these surveys are to provide insights on consumer attitudes towards financial products and services and on the factors that drive consumer behaviour. For example, the UK FCA conducts an online and face-to-face survey of UK adults called Financial Lives survey (FL survey). The first FL survey was conducted in 2017 and included a sample of 13 000 adults. The sample is representative of the UK adult population. The second, third and fourth FL surveys were conducted in 2020, 2022 and 2024, respectively (Financial Conduct Authority, 2024[15]). The Dutch AFM has been conducting a survey of financial consumers' behaviour and attitudes (Autoriteit Financiële Markten, 2021[16]).

The Consumer Protection Federal Bureau (CFPB) conducts a survey of US adults called "Making Ends Meet" to understand consumer experiences and decisions relating to financial products and services. (Consumer Financial Protection Bureau, 2023[17]). A key characteristic of the "Making Ends Meet" survey is that the survey samples are drawn from the CFPB's Consumer Credit Panel (CCP), which is a comprehensive sample of credit records maintained by one of the three nationwide consumer reporting agencies. The association with the CCP allows the CFPB to identify characteristics of individuals who do not respond to the survey and to supplement survey responses with insights on actual consumer behaviour.

The Financial Consumer Agency of Canada (FCAC) conducts a monthly Financial Well-Being Survey to gather insights on the determinants of financial well-being such as the social and economic environment, financial knowledge and experience, psychological factors, and financially capable behaviour (Financial Consumer Agency of Canada, 2024[18]).

South Africa's Financial Sector Conduct Authority released in 2023 the inaugural edition of its Financial Customer Behaviour and Sentiment Study. The study evaluates how customers engage with and perceive the financial sector in South Africa, and whether consumers' experiences indicate that financial institutions are upholding the Treating Customers Fairly (TCF) outcomes (Financial Sector Conduct Authority, 2023[19]).

3.4. Theme 4 – Informing and educating financial consumers (Principle 4)

Financially literate consumers can take more informed decisions about spending, savings and investing, increasing their financial resilience and well-being (Bottazzi and Oggero, 2023[20]; Vaahtoniemi et al., 2023[21]; OECD, 2023[22]). To help consumers develop the knowledge, skills, behaviours and attitudes to understand risks in financial markets and to make more informed choices, Principle 4 of the FCP Principles advocates for the promotion of financial literacy and awareness by all relevant stakeholders as part of a wider national financial inclusion and/or literacy strategy.

Consistent with the FCP Principles and the OECD Recommendation on Financial Literacy, Ireland's Department of Finance (DoF) is currently developing a national strategy for financial literacy (national trategy). In April 2024 the DoF published a mapping report to identify relevant stakeholders, emerging gaps and potential initiatives and outcomes to include in the national strategy (Department of Finance, 2024[23]), and the DoF plans to publish the national strategy in early 2025. The survey conducted by the DoF as part of the mapping report shows that a large number of stakeholders (44 of the 56 respondents to the survey) deliver financial education programmes to several target groups. These stakeholders include public bodies, adult education organisations, the financial services industry, charities and NGOs.

Although the Central Bank does not have an explicit statutory function relating to financial literacy and awareness, as described in section 2.4, the role played by the Central Bank in providing information to consumers within the scope of its mandate is relevant to Principle 4. As part of this role, the Central Bank co-operates with the CCPC and other stakeholders on financial literacy initiatives and regularly conducts consumer awareness and educational initiatives. Among these, the Central Bank:

- established the Consumer Hub to provide guidance on various topics and promotes the content across digital channels and media,
- publishes warnings about developments in financial services and educational resources targeted to younger people, and
- conducts public awareness campaigns and monitors the extent to which the public engages with such campaigns. For example, the Central Bank publishes warnings about developments in financial services, including scams and frauds (see section 2.4.1) and about unauthorised financial services providers (see section 2.2.8).

Moreover, the Central Bank also made changes to the Code to introduce provisions to make switching easier and undertook consumer research to understand how to make it easier for customers to compare mortgages and identify potential cost savings. The Central Bank also promoted a better switching environment in insurance markets (see section 2.5.2).

Finally, the survey conducted by the DoF in the context of the development of Ireland's national strategy, identified topics where more financial education initiatives are needed. Frauds and scams were the second most important topics identified by the respondents to the survey (62% of respondents), after digitalisation of financial services (65%). At the same time, the DoF's mapping report also showed that, despite being a priority for many stakeholders, frauds and scams were covered only by 23% of the initiatives (Department of Finance, 2024[23]).

Recommendations

Recognising that the Central Bank does not have an explicit statutory function relating to financial literacy and awareness, and in line with its mandate to ensure the proper and effective regulation of financial service providers and markets while ensuring that consumers of financial services are protected, the Central Bank should:

- Continue to collaborate and co-ordinate with other stakeholders on the development and implementation of the forthcoming National Strategy for Financial Literacy. This is important to share information and best practices across stakeholders, avoid duplication and use resources efficiently.
- Consider the use of financial literacy as a supervisory tool and conduct initiatives aimed at increasing consumers' awareness about their rights when dealing with financial services providers, for example by enhancing the Central Bank's Consumer Hub.
- Ensure that communication to consumers about financial scams and frauds remains a priority, given the increasing prevalence of scams and frauds in Ireland (as in many other jurisdictions).
- Continue to identify and seek to address impediments to consumers switching financial products (taking into account the potential benefits for consumers).

3.4.1. International experience

The practices of the Central Bank relating to the provision of information to, and raising awareness of, consumers are consistent with those of other authorities. An approach commonly used by the Central Bank and other authorities to protect consumers against frauds and scams is conducting information and awareness campaigns. Such campaigns often target certain categories of consumers that may be more vulnerable to risks.

Many jurisdictions, including Ireland, have witnessed a significant increase in the number and sophistication of financial scams and frauds. For example, the number of fraudulent payment transactions in Ireland increased by 7.7% between 2022 and 2023, from around 325 000 to around 350 000 , and fraud losses increased by 16.4% to almost EUR 100 million over the same period (Banking and Payment Federation Ireland, 2024[24]). Other countries have experienced similar trends, with fraud losses totalling more than USD 10 billion in 2023 in the US (Federal Trade Commission, 2024[25]) and over GBP 1.2 billion in the UK (UK Finance, 2024[26]).

In 2022, the Scam Prevention Research Committee, a committee established by the US Federal Trade Commission (FTC), published a report identifying the key challenges faced by oversight bodies when designing messages to prevent scams, and strategies to overcome these challenges. The research suggests that effective warnings should i) be memorable, actionable and repeated, ii) persuade consumers of the value of following the warning, iii) take into account individuals' beliefs and inner narratives, iv) be about specific types of scams or general tactics used by fraudsters, and v) be designed to work in the moment (Fletcher et al., 2024[27]).

Like other authorities, the Central Bank also publishes a list of unauthorised financial services providers (see section 2.2.8). Other examples include the FCA, which publishes a Warning List of unauthorised financial services providers. To encourage consumers to check the FCA Warning List before investing and to increase awareness about the tactics used by fraudsters to help consumers spot fraud attempts, the

FCA also launched a webpage called ScamSmart where consumers can find information related to the most common scams and the activity of the FCA. Finland's FIN-FSA publishes a list of warnings about unauthorised services providers. The webpage includes the name of the companies and a description of the concerns of the FIN-FSA (Finanssivalvonta, 2024[28]).

3.5. Theme 5 – Protecting consumers experiencing vulnerability (Principle 3 and 6)

Enhanced protection for consumers who may be experiencing vulnerability is an important element of financial consumer protection frameworks. Consumers may experience vulnerability in the context of financial transactions or be exposed to risks such as financial scams and frauds due to a combination of personal characteristics (e.g. disability, age, gender, level of education, linguistic proficiency), behavioural biases (e.g. overconfidence, information overload, impulsiveness, cognitive limitations) and market conditions (e.g. unemployment) (OECD, forthcoming[29]). Consumer vulnerability is relevant for Principle 3 (Access and Inclusion), Principle 6 (Equitable and Fair Treatment of Consumers) and Principle 12 (Complaints Handling and Redress).

Vulnerability is typically defined as an increased susceptibility to harm, rather than the actual experience of financial harm, hardship or detriment (O'Connor et al., 2019[30]). Consumer vulnerability can take different forms and being vulnerable is not a permanent state that applies to all consumers with a shared characteristic, and belonging to a certain category of consumer is not sufficient to make a consumer vulnerable (Hill and Sharma, 2020[31]). A forthcoming OECD report on understanding and responding to financial consumer vulnerability, developed via the Task Force on Financial Consumer Protection, discusses effective approaches to consumer vulnerability (OECD, forthcoming[29]).

The Central Bank has a number of mechanisms to support consumers in vulnerable circumstances. These include:

- in carrying out its sectoral risk assessment, the Central Bank considers a number of factors in assessing the impact of a particular risk, including whether consumers in vulnerable circumstances are impacted. Indicators of vulnerability can relate to factors such as language barriers, cognitive impairment, elder abuse, family or domestic violence, financial exploitation or abuse, mental illness, serious illness and/or circumstances such as bereavement, relationship breakdown or job loss.
- the Central Bank requires that firms act in the best interests of their customers and treat them fairly. Firms are required to apply this standard to all their customers, including those who are in vulnerable circumstances. The Central Bank also sets out its expectation in its Outlook reports and "Dear CEO" letters that firms consider the impact of their decisions on vulnerable customers and provide assistance where necessary.
- as part of the ongoing review of the Code, a new proposal under consideration refers to "consumers in vulnerable circumstances" to indicate a consumer that is a natural person and whose individual circumstances make them especially susceptible to harm, particularly where a regulated entity is not acting with the appropriate levels of care and vulnerable circumstances shall be construed accordingly (see, for example, section 2.1.3).
- the Code also requires that where a firm has identified that a consumer is vulnerable, it must ensure that the vulnerable consumer is provided with reasonable arrangements and/or assistance that may be necessary when dealing with the firm. As part of the review of the Code, the Central Bank published draft guidance for firms on how to approach consumers in vulnerable circumstances, including the broad range of vulnerable circumstances (Central Bank of Ireland, 2024[32]).
- in its Risk and Supervisory Outlook, the Central Bank stated that digital distribution channels may increase the risk that some consumers face financial exclusion through lower access to, and choice

of, suitable products. Moreover, as part of the revision of the Code, new requirements are proposed to require firms to ensure that digital technology to provide services is designed and implemented with a customer focus. Moreover, where firms move from traditional to digital business models, they must carefully consider customer impacts and mitigate against customer issues identified. Consumer research conducted as part of the review of the Code identified consumers' concerns about the digital transformation. These include issues related to access to basic financial services, support for consumers, appropriate use of personal data and protection in place from unfair practices when providers use new technologies that may take advantage of consumers' behaviours and biases (Central Bank of Ireland, 2024[33]).

The practices of the Central Bank relating to consumer vulnerability and the changes proposed in the review of the Code align well with the FCP Principles. The Central Bank's Guidance on Protecting Consumers in Vulnerable Circumstances (Central Bank of Ireland, 2024[32]) explicitly refers to the FCP Principles, and the definition of consumers in vulnerable circumstances included in the proposed revised Code reflects the approach of the FCP Principles. Consistent with the FCP Principles, the Central Bank highlights the importance of paying special attention to the treatment of consumers who may be in vulnerable circumstances, to ensure that they are not excluded from the financial system.

Recommendations

Given new requirements proposed as part of the review of the Consumer Protection Code (Code), the Central Bank should:

- Focus on the implementation of the new provisions of the Code by
  - developing a supervisory approach to ensure that financial services providers adapt to the new requirements and that consumers in vulnerable circumstances are treated fairly, and
  - clarifying to financial services providers how the Central Bank views their treatment of consumers in vulnerable circumstances from a risk tolerance perspective.
- Develop an evidence-based understanding of consumer vulnerability by undertaking research to identify the main drivers of vulnerability for Irish financial consumers and their prevalence. This could be done, for example, by including relevant questions in the survey about consumer behaviour and attitudes towards financial products and services of Ireland's adult population.
- Ensure regulated financial services providers continue to support consumers, especially those in vulnerable circumstances, during the digital transformation to make sure that digital tools and practices are designed and implemented with a consumer focus.

3.5.1. International experience

Protecting consumers in vulnerable circumstances is a crucial element of effective financial consumer protection regulation (see, for example, the forthcoming OECD report on understanding and responding to financial consumer vulnerability (OECD, forthcoming[29])). Like the Central Bank, several financial consumer protection oversight bodies factor in consumer vulnerability in their risk prioritisation and mitigation strategies. For example, Germany's Federal Financial Supervisory Authority (BaFin), embeds an analysis of consumers' circumstances in its supervisory strategy. This section provides examples of relevant approaches from selected jurisdictions.

Develop an evidence-based understanding of vulnerability

Several oversight bodies carry out research on consumer vulnerability (OECD, forthcoming[29]). The periodic data collections described in section 3.3 include questions to understand consumer vulnerability. For example, the Financial Consumer Agency of Canada (FCAC)'s Monthly Financial Wellbeing Monitor collects data across four categories, including financial vulnerability (Financial Consumer Agency of Canada, 2024[18]). In the Netherlands, the AFM's Consumer Monitor collects data on consumers' perception of their financial situations, for example whether consumers would be able to continue to live in their home if they lost their job or their relationship ended (see, for example, (Autoriteit Financiële Markten, 2021[16])). The US CFPB's Making Ends Meet survey collects data on financial wellbeing and whether consumers face difficulties in repaying their debts (Consumer Financial Protection Bureau, 2023[17]), and the UK FCA's Financial Lives includes questions about consumers' financial resilience.

Some financial consumer protection oversight bodies also conduct ad-hoc data collection with a focus on vulnerability. For example, in 2021 the AFM conducted exploratory work on the provision of financial products and services to Dutch consumers with a migrant background, estimated to be the 25% of the total population in 2021 and expected to increase to 36% in 2050. The AFM found that Dutch nationals with a migrant background are on average more financially vulnerable than Dutch nationals with no migrant background (Autoriteit Financiële Markten, 2021[34]).

New Zealand's Financial Markets Authority carried out a survey in 2022 to understand consumers' experiences with financial services. The survey also collected data to build demographic and psychographic profiles of a range of consumers, including adults with characteristics of vulnerability (New Zealand's Financial Markets Authority, 2022[35]).

Guidance to financial services providers on how to treat consumers in vulnerable circumstances

Like the Central Bank, other authorities have published guidance for financial services providers on how to approach consumers in vulnerable circumstances. For example, in 2021 the FCA published a Guidance for Firms on the Fair Treatment of Vulnerable Customers (Vulnerability Guidance) (Financial Conduct Authority, 2021[36]). The Vulnerability Guidance recognises that i) there may be factors limiting consumers' ability to take responsibility for their choices and decisions and that ii) consumers may have additional or different needs limiting their ability or willingness to make decisions and choices or to represent their own interests and that these consumers may be at greater risk of harm.

The Vulnerability Guidance expects financial services providers to provide their customers with a level of care that is appropriate given the characteristics of the customers. The Vulnerability Guidance also recognises that the level of care that is appropriate for vulnerable consumers may be different than for others and financial services providers should take particular care to ensure they are treated fairly. Finally, the Vulnerability Guidance sets out that individuals in senior positions have the responsibility to help create and maintain a culture that enables and supports staff to take responsibility for reducing the potential for harm to vulnerable customers.

Impact of digitalisation on access to financial products

Digitalisation of financial services and related distribution channels can create risks of excluding certain consumers from financial markets. Digitalisation can also increase consumers' exposure to frauds and scams and increase the complexity of financial products, increasing the risks that consumers purchase unsuitable products. Financial consumer protection oversight authorities address risks generated by digitalisation in various ways.

For example, in 2023 the Dutch Central Bank conducted a study on digital banking (with a focus on payment services). The study found that digitalisation made it more difficult for certain segments of the population to access and manage basic banking products. Building on the known factors leading to consumer vulnerability, the Dutch Central Bank collected data to estimate the prevalence of such factors and the difficulties faced by individuals when managing digital payment services (De Nederlandsche Bank, 2023[37]).

3.6. Theme 6 – Using data in financial consumer protection supervision (Principle 2)

The use of data is an essential component of the risk prioritisation framework of financial oversight bodies. As financial markets continue to evolve and grow in complexity, supervisory technology tools can enable oversight bodies to efficiently sift through vast amounts of information, identifying patterns and anomalies that may indicate emerging risks.

The Central Bank already uses data to support its supervisory functions, including data obtained from regular data collections from financial services providers, statistical data collections, consumer complaints data and social media monitoring (see section 2.2.5). All these data sources are used for example to inform the Central Bank's Sectoral Risk Assessment process and therefore its Sectoral Supervisory Strategies (see section 2.2.4). In addition, the Central Bank has used statistical analysis to identify unfair outcomes for consumers in specific cases, for example in the context of its work on price walking (see section 2.6.4).

Principle 2 advocates for oversight bodies to have capability, flexibility and the appropriate range of tools to carry out their functions. Technological developments may present a range of challenges for financial consumer protection oversight bodies, including ensuring that supervisory tools are adequate to supervise markets and monitor risks, that staff have the right mix of resources and capabilities (including capabilities that may not have been traditionally part of a supervisor's capability requirements) and that oversight bodies are able to understand and respond to emerging business and distribution models. The Central Bank's Data Strategy and the ongoing transformation aimed at enhancing the Central Bank's use of data described in section 2.2.5 is well aligned with the FCP Principles.

The Central Bank's strategy sets out data-related objectives such as improving organisational capabilities in the use of information in decision-making and enhancing the value of the Central Bank's work by deploying more effective and efficient tools, methods and ways of working (see section 2.2.3). Consistent with this, a key component of the Central Bank's Data Strategy is to improve the way data is used. The operating model includes both a governance and delivery structure, leveraging a cross-organisation approach.

As set out in section 2.2.5, the Central Bank ambitions to enhance its use of data to support its consumer protection supervisory functions including through evolving its use of existing data through robust data governance, new tools and capabilities, as well as through targeted additions and enhancements to the data it currently receives. This will be achieved in the context of the Central Bank's Data Strategy, as well as a broader ongoing effort to ensure that supervisory teams working to deliver across the Central Bank's mandates are able to access all the supervisory tools and services they need through a single internal system or workbench.

Recommendations

The Central Bank should:

- Continue to ensure that all information collected for financial consumer protection supervisory purposes adheres to data and governance standards in line with the wider Central Bank Data Strategy. This information should be used alongside data more broadly already available to the Central Bank and assessed to be relevant to identifying and articulating consumer protection risks. The combined sources should be presented in an easily accessible, consistent, usable, and digestible manner for relevant supervisory teams so that it can support the Central Bank's consumer protection supervisory functions in an efficient manner on an ongoing basis.
- Ensure that the functionality necessary to support the Central Bank's financial consumer protection supervisory functions is identified and incorporated in the single supervisory workbench throughout all stages of its evolution.
- Where necessary, continue to make targeted additions and refinements to the data that the Central Bank collects from financial services providers on an ongoing basis, in order to inform the Central Bank's financial consumer protection supervisory functions on a firm-specific, sectoral or cross sectoral basis.
- Continue to invest in staff training so that supervisory teams with responsibility for financial consumer protection supervision evolve their knowledge and abilities in order to support their use of the enhanced tools and increased data available to them.
- Continue to enhance the way in which data from the Central Credit Register (CCR) is used. CCR data could provide insights on risks to consumers, enhancing the Central Bank's risk identification capabilities and complement consumer research, subject to compliance with the requirements of the Credit Reporting Act and data protection legislation.

3.6.1. International experience

Effective use of data allows for more informed decision-making processes that let oversight bodies allocate resources more efficiently, focusing on areas of higher risk, fostering a more resilient financial system. Many financial consumer protection oversight bodies have invested significant resources in improving their use of data, for example by developing technology and suptech solutions to make supervisory processes more efficient. A 2021 World Bank report identifies four categories of suptech solutions: i) solutions for regulatory reporting, such as web portals, application programming interfaces (APIs), automated dataflows (ADFs), and supervision information systems (SISs) to collect, validate, and store data, ii) solutions to collect and process complaints data, particularly unstructured data, iii) solutions for non-traditional market monitoring, such as tools to monitor social media, online news and websites, and iv) solutions for document and business analysis, such as natural language processing solutions (World Bank, 2021[38]).

Although efficient use of data presents significant benefits, using data in the context of financial consumer protection supervision also comes with significant challenges, such as ensuring that the authority has adequate capabilities to efficiently use data and the need for a strong data governance, i.e. the arrangements in place to create, collect, store, use and share data.

Many public authorities including financial oversight bodies are making efforts to enhance their data governance. For example, the Bank of England has recently implemented new policies and guidance for its staff to make it easier, quicker and safer to work with and to make it easier to collect and manage data (Bank of England, 2024[39]). Moreover, the FCA is working with the Bank of England to improve data collection and regulatory reporting. In March 2024 the FCA and the BoE announced future work to ensure that data collections are proportionate and meet the needs of oversight bodies, to improve internal process for creating data collections, to create more efficient processes and support to meet regulatory obligations to make data definitions clearer and more consistent and to modernise data collection systems (Financial Conduct Authority and Bank of England, 2024[40]).

The European Central Bank is collaborating with European national central banks and commercial banks to improve the quality of data collected from financial services providers, foster co-operation between oversight bodies and industry, and reduce reporting burden. This is done by creating a common reporting dictionary called Bank's Integrated Reporting Dictionary (BIRD) to make it easier for financial services providers to understand reporting requirements (European Central Bank, 2024[41]).

Finally, many financial regulators use data on consumers' credit history and credit holdings to carry out their supervisory activity, although data protection requirements in different jurisdictions may impact what is possible for different oversight bodies. For example, the US CFPB uses its Consumer Credit Panel which includes credit records of a sample of the US population, to enhance its periodic surveys of consumer experiences and decisions relating to financial products and services. Credit files are also used to evaluate interventions (see for example the work of Peru's financial oversight body to assess the impact of financial literacy programmes (Frisancho, 2023[42])) or to provide insights on risk to consumers.

References

Australia Securities and Investment Commission (2024), *External panels*, https://asic.gov.au/about-asic/what-we-do/how-we-operate/external-panels/ (accessed on 23 June 2024). [14]

Autoriteit Financiële Markten (2021), *AFM Consumer Monitor Autumn*. [16]

Autoriteit Financiële Markten (2021), "Dutch nationals with a migration background". [34]

Bank for International Settlements (2015), *Report on the impact and accountability of banking supervision*, http://www.bis.org (accessed on 27 August 2024). [4]

Bank of England (2024), *The Bank's data and analytics strategy: a three-year roadmap*, https://www.bankofengland.co.uk/independent-evaluation-office/ieo-report-october-2023/the-banks-data-and-analytics-strategy-a-three-year-roadmap (accessed on 4 September 2024). [39]

Banking and Payment Federation Ireland (2024), *Payment Fraud Overview*. [24]

Bottazzi, L. and N. Oggero (2023), "Financial Literacy and Financial Resilience: Evidence from Italy", *Journal of Financial Literacy and Wellbeing*, Vol. 1/2, pp. 199-224, https://doi.org/10.1017/FLW.2023.10. [20]

Central Bank of Ireland (2024), *Guidance on Protecting Consumers in Vulnerable Circumstances*, https://www.oecd.org/finance/high-level-principles-on-financial-consumer-protection.htm. (accessed on 20 June 2024). [32]

Central Bank of Ireland (2024), *Internal Governance of the Central Bank of Ireland*. [2]

Central Bank of Ireland (2024), *Open & Engaged Charter*, https://www.centralbank.ie/about/open-engaged-charter (accessed on 4 September 2024). [10]

Central Bank of Ireland (2024), *Review of the Consumer Protection Code - Consumer Research Report*. [33]

Central Bank of Ireland (2023), *Review of Differential Pricing Regulations in the Private Car and Home Insurance Markets.* [3]

Central Bank of Ireland (2021), *Transforming Regulation and Supervision*, https://www.centralbank.ie/regulation/transforming-regulation-and-supervision (accessed on 27 August 2024). [1]

CGAP (2022), *Customer outcomes-based approach to consumer protection: a guide to measure outcomes*, https://www.cgap.org/research/reading-deck/customer-outcomes-based- (accessed on 4 September 2024). [9]

Consumer Financial Protection Bureau (2024), *Academic Research Council*, https://www.consumerfinance.gov/rules-policy/advisory-committees/academic-research-council/ (accessed on 23 June 2024). [13]

Consumer Financial Protection Bureau (2024), *Consumer Advisory Board*, https://www.consumerfinance.gov/rules-policy/advisory-committees/consumer-advisory-board/ (accessed on 23 June 2024). [12]

Consumer Financial Protection Bureau (2023), *Making Ends Meet in 2023.* [17]

De Nederlandsche Bank (2023), *Digitalisering van het betalingsverkeer: een uitkomst voor de één, een uitdaging voor de ander.* [37]

Department of Finance (2024), *Financial Literacy in Ireland: Evidence Base for a National Strategy*, https://www.gov.ie/pdf/?file=https://assets.gov.ie/290810/16ca8875-42db-468e-9c80-efc4c45382e8.pdf#page=null (accessed on 27 June 2024). [23]

European Central Bank (2024), *Banks' Integrated Reporting Dictionary*, https://bird.ecb.europa.eu/projectDefinition (accessed on 19 October 2024). [41]

Federal Trade Commission (2024), *As Nationwide Fraud Losses Top $10 Billion in 2023, FTC Steps Up Efforts to Protect the Public*, https://www.ftc.gov/news-events/news/press-releases/2024/02/nationwide-fraud-losses-top-10-billion-2023-ftc-steps-efforts-protect-public (accessed on 3 September 2024). [25]

Financial Conduct Authority (2024), *Annex to Rule Review Framework.* [8]

Financial Conduct Authority (2024), *Our Rule Review Framework*, https://www.fca.org.uk/publications/corporate-documents/our-rule-review-framework (accessed on 12 June 2024). [6]

Financial Conduct Authority (2024), *The Financial Lives survey*, https://www.fca.org.uk/financial-lives (accessed on 18 June 2024). [15]

Financial Conduct Authority (2021), *FG21/1 Guidance for firms on the fair treatment of vulnerable customers.* [36]

Financial Conduct Authority and Bank of England (2024), *Transforming Data Collection-response to phase two industry recommendations and future strategy.* [40]

Financial Consumer Agency of Canada (2024), *Canadians' Financial Well-being: Summary of FCAC survey findings*, https://www.canada.ca/en/financial-consumer-agency/programs/research/summary-covid-19-surveys.html#toc0 (accessed on 27 June 2024). [18]

Financial Sector Conduct Authority (2023), *South African financial customer behaviour and sentiment study*, https://www.fsca.co.za/Documents/South%20African%20Retail%20Financial%20Customer%20Behaviour%20and%20Sentiment%20Report.pdf (accessed on 27 June 2024). [19]

Finanssivalvonta (2024), *Warning lists and unauthorised service providers*, https://www.finanssivalvonta.fi/en/registers/warning-lists/ (accessed on 28 June 2024). [28]

Fletcher, E. et al. (2024), *A Review of Scam Prevention Messaging Research: Takeaways and Recommendations*, http://www.ftc.gov/olderadults. (accessed on 27 June 2024). [27]

Frisancho, V. (2023), "Spillover effects of financial education: The impact of school-based programs on parents", *Journal of Financial Literacy and Wellbeing*, Vol. 1/1, pp. 138-153, https://doi.org/10.1017/FLW.2023.2. [42]

Hilbers, P. et al. (2013), "Measuring the effects of supervision in the financial sector", *DNB Working Paper*. [5]

Hill, R. and E. Sharma (2020), "Consumer Vulnerability", *Journal of Consumer Psychology*, https://doi.org/10.1002/jcpy.1161. [31]

Mayne, J. (2012), "Contribution analysis: Coming of age?", *Evaluation*, Vol. 18/3, pp. 270-280, https://doi.org/10.1177/1356389012451663. [7]

New Zealand's Financial Markets Authority (2022), *Consumer Experience with the Financial Sector Survey*, https://www.fma.govt.nz/library/research/consumer-experience-research-2022/ (accessed on 2 September 2024). [35]

Newbury, L. and E. Duflos (2022), *Consumer Advisory Panels - A tool to elevate the collective consumer voice in financial sector regulation and supervision*. [11]

O'Connor, G. et al. (2019), "Conceptualizing the multiple dimensions of consumer financial vulnerability", *Journal of Business Research*, Vol. 100, pp. 421-430, https://doi.org/10.1016/J.JBUSRES.2018.12.033. [30]

OECD (2023), *OECD/INFE 2023 International Survey of Adult Financial Literacy*, https://doi.org/10.1787/56003a32-en. [22]

OECD (forthcoming), *Understanding and responding to financial consumer vulnerability*. [29]

UK Finance (2024), *Fraud remains a major problem as over £1 billion is stolen by criminals in 2023*, https://www.ukfinance.org.uk/news-and-insight/press-release/fraud-remains-major-problem-over-ps1-billion-stolen-criminals-in (accessed on 3 September 2024). [26]

Vaahtoniemi, S. et al. (2023), "Financial literacy and its determinants and consequences: New survey evidence from Finland", *Journal of Financial Literacy and Wellbeing*, Vol. 1/2, pp. 368-402, https://doi.org/10.1017/FLW.2023.14. [21]

World Bank (2021), *The Next Wave of Suptech Innovation*. [38]

www.ingramcontent.com/pod-product-compliance
Lightning Source LLC
Chambersburg PA
CBHW061223240926
51846CB00006B/1335
* 9 7 8 9 2 6 4 9 2 4 0 5 5 *